TALKING OF CONFLICT:
Christian reflections in the context of
Israel and Palestine

Edited by Jane Clements
With a Foreword by Professor Lord Harries of Pentregarth

FODIP (the Forum for Discussion of Israel and Palestine) seeks to promote sensitive and productive inter religious dialogue in the context of the Israeli/Palestinian situation.
- www.fodip.org -
Office: 52 Cornmarket Street,
Oxford OX1 3HJ
Reg. charity no. 1139005
Company no. 07343229
Reg. office address Star House 104 Grafton Road, London NW4 5BA

Copyright © 2012 Jane Clements

The moral right of the author has been asserted.

Apart from any fair dealing for the purposes of research or private study, or criticism or review, as permitted under the Copyright, Designs and Patents Act 1988, this publication may only be reproduced, stored or transmitted, in any form or by any means, with the prior permission in writing of the publishers, or in the case of reprographic reproduction in accordance with the terms of licences issued by the Copyright Licensing Agency. Enquiries concerning reproduction outside those terms should be sent to the publishers.

Matador
9 Priory Business Park
Kibworth Beauchamp
Leicestershire LE8 0RX, UK
Tel: (+44) 116 279 2299
Fax: (+44) 116 279 2277
Email: books@troubador.co.uk
Web: www.troubador.co.uk/matador

ISBN 978 1780881 041

British Library Cataloguing in Publication Data.
A catalogue record for this book is available from the British Library.

Typeset in 10.5pt Bembo by Troubador Publishing Ltd, Leicester, UK

Matador is an imprint of Troubador Publishing Ltd

Printed and bound in the UK by TJ International, Padstow, Cornwall

Contents

List of Contributors	vi
A word about this volume	x
Foreword, *Richard Harries*	xii
Introduction, *Jane Clements*	xiv
Who says who is right & wrong in a conflict? The Victim-Perpetrator-Cycle of the Israel-Palestine Conflict, *Shanthikumar Hettiarachchi*	1
Jerusalem in Imagination and Reality, *Mark Chapman*	27
Conflict and Religion, *Douglas Hedley*	49
The Language of Politics and the Language of the Cross, *Patrick Riordan*	64
I Am – For You, *Clare Amos*	86
Bibliography	103

List of Contributors

Mrs **Clare Amos** is Programme Executive for Interreligious Dialogue and Cooperation at the World Council of Churches. Until recently she was Director of Theological Studies in the Anglican Communion Office, where she held responsibility for theological education and inter faith concerns. Clare is a lecturer in biblical studies by background and has lived and worked in both Jerusalem and the Lebanon. Her commentary on Genesis (for the Epworth series) takes as its starting point the need to read Genesis is a way that allows the concerns of Palestinians (particularly Palestinian Christians) to be heard.

Professor **Mark Chapman** is Vice-Principal and Dean of Residential Students at Ripon College Cuddesdon where he has taught for the past eighteen years. He teaches modern Church History and theology. He is Reader in Modern Theology in the University of Oxford, Visiting Professor at Oxford Brookes University, as well as associate priest in Garsington, Horspath and Cuddesdon. He has written and edited books in many different areas of theology and church history. His most recent book is *Doing God: Religion and Public Policy in Brown's Britain* (DLT, 2008). He is also author of *Anglicanism: A Very Short Introduction* (OUP, 2006).

Dr **Jane Clements** is the Founder and Director of the Forum for Discussion of Israel and Palestine (FODIP), a registered charity which facilitates conversations between faith communities in the UK on this issue. An Anglican, Jane has worked in interreligious dialogue as advisor and practitioner for more than ten years, including extensive work on the Israeli/Palestinian conflict. Her recent publications include in (eds.) Smith & Rittner *No Going Back: Letters to Pope Benedict XVI on the Holocaust, Jewish-Christian Relations and Israel.*

Dr **Douglas Hedley** is Fellow of Clare College and Reader in Hermeneutics and Metaphysics in the Faculty of Divinity at the University of Cambridge. His publications include *Coleridge, Philosophy and Religion* (Cambridge 2000) and *Living Forms of the Imagination* (Continuum, 2008).

Dr **Shanthikumar Hettiarachchi** holds a PhD in majority-minority ethnic and religious conflict, Melbourne College of Divinity, University of Melbourne and lectures in Religion, Conflict and Social cohesion. He has worked extensively with community groups and social movements in Sri Lanka and studied them at depth. His primary research interests are in the Diaspora communities – their settlement processes, religious affiliations, mobilisation, identity politics in social and cultural adjustments in the UK, Europe and Australia – and his writings dwell on radicalization of religious faith, land, history and notions of chosen-ness as political tools to define identity. His most recent involvement has been in the rehabilitation and de-radicalisation of ex-combatants in Sri Lanka's post conflict period.

Dr **Patrick Riordan SJ** teaches political philosophy at Heythrop College, University of London. His research interests are Religion in Public Life, the Philosophy of Justice, and the Common Good. His publications include *A Grammar of the Common Good: Speaking of Globalization* (Continuum, 2008), and *Values in Public Life: Aspects of Common Goods* (editor) (LIT Verlag, 2007). Among his recent articles are: 'Talk and Terror: the Value of Just-War

Arguments in the Context of Terror', in: *Israel, Palestine and Terror* (Continuum, 2008); 'Five Ways of Relating Religion and Politics or Living in Two Worlds, Believer and Citizen' in *The New Visibility of Religion. Studies in Religion and Cultural Hermeneutics* (Continuum 2008); and 'Doing Business for the Common Good? Lessons from the Credit Crisis', in *Ethics in Economic Life: Challenges to a Globalizing World* (Innsbruck University Press, 2009).

A word about this volume

In the course of Christian discussions about the Israeli Palestinian conflict, there often comes a call for 'more theological reflection'. Unfortunately, in some cases this is used as just another way into the same argument, through theological terminology or by attacking certain positions. There are a number of recognisable theological 'Aunt Sallys' which some Christian writers choose to address simply in order to knock them down.

This book starts from a totally different perspective. It began life under the direction of the Forum for Discussion of Israel and Palestine (FODIP), a faith-based charity facilitating dialogue between Jews, Christians and Muslims on this divisive issue. The project brought together a working group of five scholars from different theological fields, but all with an interest in the criteria Christians may use in talking about conflict in general and the Israeli Palestinian situation in particular. Each contributor has brought his or her own area of expertise to the subject matter. What has emerged is a collection of papers with fresh areas of consideration and stimulating invitations to continue the conversation. It should be made very clear that this is *not* a book about the Israeli Palestinian conflict; rather, it is an exploration of the tools Christians might and do use to talk about it.

It became clear early on in our discussions that issues of language, and how we choose to speak about the conflict, are of central importance. We asked the question: how is it possible to have dialogue, when the very ways in which we speak about the conflict feed the problem? So often our discussions become the obstacle to change – change which so many of us long to see. Moreover, such discussions can polarise the Christian world, let alone hinder our dealings with our Jewish and Muslim cousins.

FODIP was founded on the premise that, unless and until we can learn to speak together profitably, for purposes of understanding and cooperation, we are condemned to replicate the conflict in our own societies and in our own places of worship. Only by learning to work and talk together for the good of others, even where there are fundamental disagreements about the causes, can we hope to be of use to the people of the region. This slim volume is simply an invitation to continue the dialogue, avoiding the hackneyed clichés and the well-rehearsed rhetoric, and to seek new, creative ways to engage. Its contributors have experience and committed interest in these issues and I hope that something within these pages will strike a definite chord with each reader.

In bringing these thoughts to publication, thanks must be expressed particularly to Revd Dr Jenny Gaffin, who coaxed the papers into a semblance of order, and to the Sir Halley Stewart Trust for their invaluable support in getting the project started.

Jane Clements
Oxford
2011

FOREWORD

Talking of conflict

Richard Harries

I was fortunate enough to spend a term as a student at St George's College in East Jerusalem, which was then under the protection of Jordan. We also spent time in Israel. Jerusalem was then divided by barbed wire, and there were pock marks on the walls made by bullets in the recent conflict. The atmosphere was tense. That was 1962. But if the issue seemed tragic and difficult then, it seems even more intractable now. It is extraordinary to think that since that time the Cold War, which I thought would continue for a hundred years or more, has ended. Apartheid, which I thought could only end in a terribly bloody revolution, ended peacefully. Yet the conflict between Israel and Palestine, where a workable agreement has been on the cards for so long, seems even further from ending.

In this situation we need all the light we can, and that is why I very much welcomed FODIP when it was founded. For I had discovered during my time as Chairman of The Council of Christians and Jews, that for all the progress that has been made on Jewish Christian relations since World War II, Israel is still very much a sore place in the dialogue. Christians are divided in their approach to this issue, as indeed in a different way, are Jews. This is why I also welcome *Talking of Conflict,* with its variety of approaches to the subject, and its reminder that all words used in discussing it are weighted with history and emotion.

It is said that during the time of the Italian Renaissance and the conflict between city states, one prince said to another "We understand each other perfectly. We both want Italy." That might be taken as a warning about the limits of mere understanding. But it can also be taken as a call to try to understand more deeply, to understand from the standpoint of the other, to look from different angles. This book seeks to help this process.

Richard Harries
(Professor Lord Harries of Pentregarth)

INTRODUCTION

In the beginning were the words: using the language of the conflict

Jane Clements

At a seminar in London, a young man listened intently to a variety of presentations on Christian approaches to the Israeli/Palestinian conflict.

When it came time for questions, he asked simply: "well, who started it?" Somewhat taken aback, the speaker responded, "why do you ask that?" The young man replied, "Because if we knew who started it, we would know how to end it."

This exchange, with a whole raft of historical and theological implications lurking behind it, highlights some of the problems involved in talking about this highly contested subject. One may marvel at the simplicity of this young man's approach. Those of us familiar with discussion on this topic will know that there is no face-value answer one can begin to give to such as question as 'how did it all start?' which will not be loaded with assumptions and omissions, whoever we are. And even though many people believe they could answer that question, we are all left with the follow-on 'but what happens next?' What we have in terms of the Israel/Palestinian situation is so much history, so many stories of suffering and so much misplaced international interference.

One of the major problems in forming any sort of consensus – both for ourselves or internationally – hinges on the very nature of communication. How we choose to speak about the conflict is, of course, far from straightforward. There are as many narratives as there are speakers, with use of language – vocabularies and even the topics we choose to introduce – highly contentious and often divisive. We are very familiar with approaches to this subject, especially in the media, where each phrase is strongly contested by one group or another, and with paragraphs and articles regularly denounced as being inaccurate, biased and even inflaming the conflict itself. An email correspondence, which arrived in the FODIP office in Spring of 2011, included a description of a meeting held in a church:

'The talk I attended was riddled with misinformation and prejudice. [The speaker] finished the talk with a picture of "Eretz Israel"[1] which she kept as the backdrop during questions. This picture came from a holocaust denying, anti-Semitic website with Eretz Israel taking on unbelievable dimensions. She said that this was what all Israelis want because it says so in the Bible! The talk was delivered in an angry and emotive fashion which whipped everybody up. When the small number of Jews in the audience got up and tried to balance, for example, the history, they were heckled and booed. The atmosphere allowed even clergy in the audience to vent their anti-Semitic prejudices.' *(Private correspondence, unpublished.)*

One is in no position to judge whether or not this was an accurate account, but there is no doubting the hurt and concern of the writer and, unfortunately, such occasions are not uncommon. Those of us with considerable experience in ecumenical, inter faith or cross-cultural discussions know that true dialogue does not encourage such destructive approaches. Dialogue of the more productive kind is about listening rather than speaking; it requires a desire to understand one's dialogue partner a little better and acknowledges the willingness of those involved to be challenged, even changed a little, by the experience. Those who enter into dialogue on the Israeli/Palestinian situation may often do so with similar desires. It is, however, important to understand the pitfalls which await us in this.

We rarely have the time – or, sometimes, the incentive – to consider that whatever we are seeing, reading and hearing about the conflict takes root in our minds through a series of filters and channels, gathering concepts and beliefs and half-grasped information and prejudices on its way. If we are interested in making any sort of progress in terms of gaining a fuller picture of what is happening and of understanding nuances and different perspectives, we must first consider what can be said in terms of our 'reading and receiving' process; that is, how we understand the language of the conflict debate.

Taking a moment to consider how we speak about anything can be useful in understanding how to engage in dialogue. Language has been described as the process whereby meaning is constructed, as a result of experiences and discussions[2]; there is no objectivity of meaning, since all knowledge is socially and historically specific. The French semiologist Roland Barthes wrote about 'cultural mythologies', by which an entire association of meaning accompanies any given word and can be implicitly understood by those familiar with that culture. How we use and understand key concept words and phrases not only derives from a shared culture but also serves to reinforce it, by its shared use. The word 'Israel' is, as it happens, a strong example of this, since its use brings with it a raft of cultural and religious assumptions, dependent upon who is speaking and hearing. When we enter into a discussion with others on the Israeli/Palestinian conflict, the words we use are invested for us with layers of meaning; the likelihood is, however, that these will be different for each individual involved.

It may be arguable, but I think it is fair to say that most attitudes of those in Britain and the USA towards Israel and its inhabitants are largely composed of a number of such frameworks of thought. When a label is affixed to anyone ('pro-Palestinian',

'Christian Zionist' or whatever), we then expect to know their views on a whole range of issues relating to the Middle East – and they may even be judged accordingly. To develop an approach to the Israeli Palestinian conflict which does not conform to any recognisable framework of thought is difficult. It is often even more difficult to convince others that you have done so. This is because such frameworks comprise attitudes and approaches which are both described by the vocabulary of its 'community', but which are also, in effect, developed and sustained by it. Those who adopt a given framework of speech – and thought – reinforce the framework constantly, by reciting and expounding on it. Thus each person is judged as being 'one of us' or 'one of them'; he who is not for us is against us.

Michel Foucault used the term 'discourse' to describe such methods of social practice, as well as commonly held beliefs and attitudes. A community not only holds to its own discourse but also reinforces it, through behaviour and vocabulary. The discourse may add some features over time and discard others; it is a fluid process, constructed to be of use to its own community. A discourse not only enables a social group to talk about a subject, but it also serves to define the parameters of attitude and behaviour shared by the group. In the context of the Israeli Palestinian situation, this is how views become polarised. Individuals listen to those statements which resonate most closely with their acquired approaches, adopt them, reinforce them and help to redefine them as part of a discursive community.

Discourses may also be described as having a *repressive* function – not in any negative or judgmental way – as the limits of the discourse not only reinforce those elements which serve and feed the purpose and nature of the discourse; they also exclude those elements which are seen as being in opposition to or not concerned with it. Unfortunately, this increases the risk of those who hold to a particular position going out of their way to avoid hearing the voices of others. Discursive communities often have a tendency to wear their allegiances as 'badges', perhaps even challenging concessions made towards other perspectives. Anyone who is part of a social group which has a shared discourse will be most likely to conform to its discursive formations, and may even contribute to its development and sustainability. We feel most comfortable among those who share our perceptions, and we may naturally gravitate towards them.

Not all discourses are negative and polarising, and these may be the ones with which Christians consciously want to engage. These include discourses of reconciliation or peaceful, even creative resistance. The particular challenge for exponents of these, however, is the avoidance of becoming part of another discursive community which refuses to listen. The most successful *dialoguers* are those who confound expectations or who allow themselves to be challenged. These are usually the very people who can help to move a dialogue on a little, enabling it to grow in new and positive directions.

In contrast, too many discussions, unfortunately, seem to comprise apparently objective content wherein 'facts' are traded between members of different camps. The enclosure of the word 'facts' here in inverted commas is not to suggest that there are not real, historical events involved in the conflict, but that the statements used in these exchanges are often intended as artillery fire to quash the opponent and to win the argument. They may also be familiar well-rehearsed phrases. Like most of the arguments presented in the theological disputations of medieval times, they are grounded in the discourses which are only of authority to the community from which they originate.

There are important reasons why Christians do and should engage with this issue; one major reason is that it involves other Christians. The indigenous Christian Palestinians – an early and once thriving part of the Body of Christ – are the forgotten casualties in the

Israeli/Palestinian conflict. Wholly Palestinian, these are 'the same, but different', as they suffer hardships and privations together with their Muslim compatriots. There are other, less well-established Christian congregations in the region; the more recently arrived Christian Israeli presence includes converts, Western Christians and immigrants from the former Soviet Union. The Church as a whole has a responsibility to hear these voices and to act as appropriate.

It is not, of course, very easy to differentiate facts ('what exactly *did* happen in 1948?') from the discourse, and sometimes Christians are disinclined to do so; it is far easier to reject any facts which other discourses may present as being mere propaganda. The objectivity of the events should be viewed separately from the way in which many current disputations are conducted, even in some cases involving rituals and ideologies of their own. How we choose to speak about the conflict is essentially creative; while the content may be factual, its presentation involves language which is itself descriptive and subjective.

Equally important is what is *not* being said. When someone speaks or responds with emotion, we must learn to listen for what is really being expressed, deriving from the experiences and approaches of the individual before engaging in a superficial way with the words themselves. *Advices and Queries,* in the Quaker Faith and Practice guidelines, counsels:

> "When words are strange or disturbing to you, try to sense where they come from and what has nourished the lives of others. Listen patiently and seek the truth which other people's opinions may contain for you. Avoid hurtful criticism and provocative language. Do not allow the strength of your convictions to betray you into making statements or allegations that are unfair or untrue. Think it possible that you may be mistaken."

The Christian template for communication is immensely powerful. In the Incarnation of the Word we witness challenging but transforming approaches in terms of engaging with humanity. 'The Word became flesh and dwelt among us': this is the most dramatic element and the most effective, whereby the Divine was revealed and could be understood at a profound level. To follow this example, Christians must recognise a moral imperative to desire to enter into a relationship with humanity – to both understand and, wherever possible, to be a catalyst for change. Transformative change is the goal of Christian activity.

In Jesus' dealings with individuals we find further illumination on this point. The gospels present Jesus as recognising the constraints and background of the person with whom he is in conversation, and tailoring his demands of them accordingly. Both the gospels and Acts also demonstrate an awareness of modes of address. The writers, as with the preachers they describe, know or imagine their audience and design the message to connect directly.

It is my contention that Christians who engage in 'successful dialogue' have endeavoured to follow this example. It may also be that they have understood on some level the importance of two principles. The first principle is a unified theology of God, humanity and the Kingdom. In the varied disputations about Israel and Palestine that go on between different members of religious groups, there comes a point when people refer to what is, for them, some sort of 'bottom line'. While the main substance of such disputations is concerned with apparent 'facts' – what happened when, who started what and, most importantly, who has the capacity to create the greatest havoc – the 'bottom line' always comprises a non-negotiable set of values. One challenge for Christians is to ensure that these values are firmly rooted within a framework of theology which takes account of issues such as incarnation, redemption and establishing the Kingdom of God – theology which seeks the ultimate wellbeing of all through *agape* love.

Stanley Hauerwas, in his autobiography, underlines his concern that ethics should not be 'divorced' from theology (2010, p.115): "I realize that many who want to maintain the independence of Christian ethics would protest that "divorce" is too strong a word. But too often it accurately describes how ethics is done. Love or justice or some other fundamental principle is identified with *the* source of the moral life. God and the church might be assumed as background beliefs that may be needed to sustain the intelligibility of the fundamental principle or principles, but they are seldom thought to be vital to how our lives are constituted." Hauerwas is clear that our ethical selves must be integrated with our liturgical, intellectual selves. The desire for justice (or peace, or security of others) alone is not enough; it must arise from a theological imperative in keeping with our life and worship.

Especially enticing in this regard is the demand for justice. Derived from the Hebrew scriptures, the imperative of the prophetic vision is reinforced in the gospels. And yet, when we look at things from an integrated theological perspective, we must acknowledge that *change* is the goal of Christian activity. Perhaps we need to ask ourselves questions which suppose answers of success: what does our understanding of God lead us to expect us to do? What paths does he require us to walk, and how will we deal with the challenges they present to us? What will sustain us on our way and how will we know when we have completed the task? When we start to think in these terms, we begin to enter the world of the real and the practical, and to recognise that what one needs to achieve for the sake of both Palestinians and Israelis is not about any sort of wishful thinking, but about real milestones in making a difference. To do that, we need to understand what each side seeks: what are the needs of each which must be met before we can consider whether we are helping the process?

These questions may lead to some unsettling answers, but the second principle involved in useful dialogue is that of 'uncomfortableness'. When Jesus challenged people in the gospels, he often invited them to feel uncomfortable about themselves and their relationship with God and the world. Such an uncomfortableness requires one to feel the ground shift a little, perhaps to be less sure or convinced, or for prejudices to be challenged. Being saddened or angered on behalf of others is not the same thing; this is about understanding something very differently from one's usual approach to life. Such reflection may even involve an interrogation of one's perception of self in terms of desires and goals – whatever is required in order to reach a unified theological approach of God, humanity and the Kingdom.

Desiring to consider issues of conflict in this context, the papers in this volume derive from reflections and discussions between scholars from five different disciplines. Each paper suggests a framework from Christian tradition which may offer new insights on ways forward – involving love, vision, inner transformation, the Way of the Cross and the encounter with the 'I Am'.

Shanthikumar Hettiarachchi presents both the rationale and the imperative for this engagement. For people of all faiths and none, identification with one side or another in the conflict can provide a form of moral escapism; one may feel part of the universal struggle for 'good' through such vicarious involvement. Uncompromisingly, Hettiarachchi calls for a realistic view of each side's situation, which is not obscured by the simplistic labels of victim and perpetrator. To embrace the offender is, he points out, the "fundamental obligation" of the Christian, whose task as peacemakers is derived "from the practice of Jesus in the Gospel, where there is no compromise for reconciliation and forgiveness". Sometimes, in the voices raised in the churches in favour of boycotts and exclusions and condemnations, there may also be discerned not just a very real and 'human' aversion to embrace the offender, but even a desire to punish – to 'make them learn' through the medium of harsh words or treatment. But Hettiarachchi challenges Christians, not to remain standing on the moral high ground, but to descend and be "flexible conduits generating transparent engagement [as stewards] for a cordially coded agreement to live in peace".

While many would and do want to visit the Land itself, the question of 'pilgrimage' is now more complex than it once was. Rather than visiting 'holy places', the work of Living Stones and the theology of the Sabeel Centre have partly redefined it as an opportunity for engagement with oppressed Palestinian Christians. Mark Chapman, in his chapter on Jerusalem, opens up some of the complexities involved in an approach which may be both spiritual and incarnational. He argues for pilgrimage as a religious experience, which "takes the lives of contemporary people seriously, and which sees them all as created in the image of God". Furthermore, he underlines the fact that "conversation is rooted in the doctrine of incarnation: the ideal and the real co-exist in the act of remembering in the present for the sake of the future".

Douglas Hedley takes incarnation a step further in his paper, considering what may be involved in being human. In discussing the relationship between a religious approach to life and conflict, Hedley argues for religion as a means of addressing the human tendency to violence. In the case of the 'Holy Land', he points out the need for Christianity, Islam and Judaism to find a way to support a mutual flourishing, involving a process of reconciliation which, in its turn, requires both forgiveness and justice. In the quest for peace, Hedley observes that the necessary transformation of humanity can only be achieved through the action of the Divine, since "the human heart is not only restless, but deeply conflicted".

How we attempt to describe and thereby 'manage' conflict is further explored in Patrick Riordan's paper which highlights the poverty of religious language in particular: "The language of values and ideals is aspirational, and it is not necessarily helpful for managing conflict." Conflict as such is found in many areas of both personal and social life, and we spend a great deal of time at both levels holding competing values in tension; such management is part of the language of politics, as Riordan describes it. While Riordan is critical of the use of religious language partly because of its partisan appeal, he nevertheless makes a compelling argument for both the symbolism and reality of the Cross as a vehicle for addressing non-violent management- and understanding – of conflict. As he makes clear, there is a distinction drawn here between language which communicates a shared world view, as in the frameworks explored above, and language which speaks across boundaries. In times and places of conflict the former may tend to obfuscate, but the latter may illuminate.

Above all, as Christians, our understanding of humanity is a reflection of how we understand God. Taking a passage of conflict in John 8, Clare Amos explores the notion of a God who seeks definition as 'I am who I am'. God *is* only in relation to humanity, as Amos underlines through narratives of encounter with Moses, Jacob and the Samaritan woman at the well. If we can truly understand what it means for us to relate to God, who defies all attempts to be confined linguistically, then perhaps we can begin to relate to those who are other to us.

---

[1] *Hebrew*: 'the land of Israel'

[2] "Meanings are born of co-ordinations among persons – agreements, negotiations, affirmations. From this standpoint, relationships stand prior to all that is intelligible." Gergen (1999, p.48)

Who says who is right & wrong in a conflict? The Victim-Perpetrator-Cycle of the Israel-Palestine Conflict

Shanthikumar Hettiarachchi

Foreword

Conflicts have always been a challenging reality of all human communities. They often emerge as a result of a response to oppressive regimes, to bring order in society.

The recently defeated Tamil Tigers[3] in Sri Lanka claimed that they represented the sole ethnic Tamil voice to bring order to their community and to regain the rights denied by the majority-Sinhala-dominated governments. The secessionist conflict might have come to an end, but some other conflict is looming after the defeat of the Tamil Tigers on this island nation. The world community is watching the next move by the rulers and the ruled of that fragile democracy, which is symbolic of all conflicts and their aftermath contexts.

The expansionist or secessionist agendas, majority-minority fears, lack of opportunities to make a decent living, trade, economics and clamour for resources have also been the origins of conflict in many parts of the world. Hence, a homogenisation of religion and the modus operandi of conflicts differ a great deal from one to another. Each must be dealt within in its own context, considering its geopolitical parameters and historical perspectives. Their complexity cannot be underestimated in seeking for a negotiated solution, peace building and the long-drawn-out process of reconciliation and healing of memories. It is in this sense that one wonders whether this history of humanity has been a history of conflict. Eric Hobsbawm looks at this in his fourth of 'The Age Of' series[4], *The Age of Extremes* (1995), where he invites twelve other scholars and Nobel peace Laureates to look at the twentieth century, where all of them refer to it as a century of conflicts. René Dumont, an agronomist and ecologist, states that it is a "century of massacres and wars," and for William Golding, Nobel Laureate and writer, "it is a 'most violent century in human history," while Isaiah Berlin, British philosopher says "…. I remember it only as the most terrible century in Western history" (Hobsbawm 1995, p.1).

Winds of Change in Conflict

It is also a fact that all conflict situations in the past have been dealt with by the mechanisms available to that specific time and the understanding of how to resolve them at that point in history. Hence, as much as humans have initiated conflict, they have also been the agents to resolve such conflicts. They possess both skills, able to spark conflicts quite destructively while able to find solutions which obviously may take years of negotiations, rebuilding and healing of communities. However, conflicts do not arise like a spout of water in a lush valley and neither do they fade away like a withering flower; hence societies cannot afford to prolong conflict resolution. Procrastination of solutions, like a wheel to a bullock cart, drag the conflict along, solidifying it into disproportionate and intractable positions.

Hobsbawm, in his 'Age Of Series', resourcefully expands the vivid sense of history. However, his fourth exploration is helpful to the current discussion as this paper identifies three significant historical endings and a beginning[5] that have serious implications to most contemporary conflicts which include the Israel-Palestine conflict as well. Every ending gave a glimpse of hope yet led to several other situations of conflict. The end of World War II provided a breathing space to understand and find some way to cope with the most horrific human cruelty to fellow human beings in epic proportions. Secondly, the consequences of this War and the winds of freedom wrapped in nationalist garb paved the way to the break up of the colonial regimes in the global South. Thirdly, the actual fall of the Berlin Wall and its symbolism as ending the Cold War, was a breath of fresh air that many thought might also be the end of most conflicts that have been around in the twentieth century. Fourthly, the Beginning of the War on Terror, which also was engrossed in geopolitical and economic disparities, was sparked by the triumph of political and economic liberalism,[6] its universalisation and the subtle imposition of it on the rest of the world, which was unwilling to accommodate it uncritically. The Kashmir dispute and Israel-Palestine are the longest conflicts. The Kashmir issue is currently dormant, while the latter remains the most protracted issue, and has failed to resolve, though many have attempted to find a mutually acceptable solution. It is a fact that both remain conflicts which are the residue of colonial political arrangements that have been derailed in their operational apparatus, and continue to infuse dysfunctional geopolitical behaviour with many manifestations to different people at different times.

Mother of all Conflicts?

What makes the Israel-Palestine dispute so deeply entrenched is that it is fought within its own terrain and in distant theatres with ideological fronts evoked by the militant 'Zionist' and 'Islamist' political agendas. The Al Qaeda and other similar religio-politically motivated 'Jihadi militants' have embraced the protracted Middle Eastern issue and given their own combatant interpretation and the justification for militant engagement. Hence, some tend to argue that the Israel-Palestine conflict is the 'mother of all conflicts', which in my view is an exaggerated slogan as every conflict is contextual in terms of its origin, history and how each has evolved, calcified and protracted. The two best examples are the Northern Ireland and the Tamil Tiger contexts, in Western Europe and South Asia. Each of their tactical involvements has attracted sympathisers, a strategic Diaspora political energy,[7] external funders and intellectual acumen across the world, internationalising the conflict itself. The protracted nature of the Israel-Palestine conflict and its links to a historical and sacralised piece of land, each claiming ownership with an unalienable right to exist has rendered the dispute acutely deplorable with ordinary people in both camps having to live in constant fear of being attacked.

What the Jews and Palestinians desire for this piece of land is yet another big question, when both communities are so deeply fractured after all the years of bitter fighting. The internal divisions (ad intra)[8] are possibly the major factor to be resolved, as well as the deep rooted suspicions between the so called 'Israelis and Palestinians' (ad extra)[9].

Christians amidst the Conflict

After seeing decades of occupation, discrimination, dispossession, violence and bloodshed in Israel-Palestine territories, it appears to be a theological obligation for Christians to study and reflect critically on the question of 'Sacred land' and other religio-political claims and be challenged in order to promote the offer of life affirming Christian vision. Is the preferential option of the international community for the Palestinians to exist in their land, and the Israelis also to live with security? Israel has argued that that they live with terror in their front yard. For people to live in security and peace is a matter which all those engaged in conflict resolution should fundamentally recognize and bring into their discourse and dialogue processes, side by side with whatever political arrangements are to be negotiated. Theology based on preferential option in this conflict can also be a subscription to a partisan politics by certain groups and this tendency indicates the entrenched nature of the crisis. It is a fact that at several points, Christians, Muslims and Jews are painfully aware that each group has differing interpretations, contexts, perspectives, interests, solidarities and antagonisms towards each other. They all have camps of companions and supporters in the rest of the world over the issue of territoriality and the sacred claim to land. The Worldwide cousins of the three faiths seem to have also brought back their medieval antagonisms now compounded with the rhetoric of war against terror, with Islam and Muslims as the newest threat to modernity. Others believe that the return to medieval antagonisms would be to turn blind eye to the potential human progress and the development of thought achieved since the Enlightenment.[10]

Time is running out for ordinary people who are caught up in the middle of the conflict, hence the need to search for a political solution that has implications for Jewish-Christian-Muslim religious traditions. All three faiths are involved in this land made '(un)holy.' They need to re-examine the notions of the 'Promised Land' critically and creatively in textual traditions, myths and legends which in fact are the burdens of history and the legacy of enmity. The Jews and Christians on theological grounds, and the Jews and Muslims on the political stage have to harness their energy, if they all wish to be secure and become rightful heirs to a truly 'holy land'. What they have lost is probably unrecoverable. They all have to cope with the shame of their disobedience to the moral and ethical living, which is based on their deeply revelatory and scriptural backgrounds, as well as what has shaped their civilizations and praxis. Christians and their theological traditions do possess and could propose conciliatory thinking towards the healing process even though they are all part of the problem. This should indeed be part of the solution to the Israel-Palestine crisis.

A Christian Response

What can the Christians derive from their own text, the Bible, which contains a variety of topics – God's promises, the land, the Abraham paradigm, the Church and Israel, and the people of God? It is a fact that the Christians across denominational boundaries have witnessed the transformative and incisive character of encounters among Christians holding vastly different views on this crisis. It begins from the crucial issue among Christians: how the Bible is read[11]. It is paramount that Christians, as they are called upon to understand the text and the context of their interpretations, that they acknowledge the differences between the modern State of Israel[12] and the history of Israel in the biblical story[13]. These overviews would help many to familiarise themselves with the biblical, philosophical, historical and cultural nuances as well as the idioms of pronouncements, actions and their ethical implications. Such an approach can in fact shed light on the analysis of the ground situation and engage critically with the notions of Antisemitism, Islamophobia, Zionism, Christian Evangelicalism and the Jihadist agenda which are at the core of the conflict. Each of the Abrahamic faiths holds on to an assertive rhetoric which becomes perceptively 'holier than thou'.

The sheer breadth of the conflicts and the violence we know today from Mindanao to Israel-Palestine whether they be political, ethnic or territorial, are cocooned in a web of complexity. Each of their contextual situations and history of origins lends to their prolongation. The Christians, Muslims and other religious traditions have no choice but to respond to these very unpalatable exigencies to make sense of what they profess as to what is right and wrong, to recapture a moral compass with dignity and integrity. What motivates Christians to contribute to conflict resolution processes in places where they are actively present and to steer through reconciliation and forgiveness in the aftermath of such conflicts? They draw their reason for engagement from the practice of Jesus in the Gospel, where there is no compromise for reconciliation and forgiveness. It is a deeply spiritual willingness to agree to do business as reasonable human being with agility, fairness and honesty.

These are not exclusively Christian propositions. However it becomes clearer for Christians that they experience and desire to live the witness of their model of the praxis of reconciliation and forgiveness. The Christians, like many others, have some hurdles to cross. Firstly, the fear of being inundated with the sheer inability to heal memories of the past caused by the wrongdoers or the perpetrators. Secondly, the other fear of appearing to be weak, the feeling of the possible betrayal of the cause and having to be seen helpless and vulnerable. But the wrongdoers will continue with their aggression. Thirdly, there is yet another fear of dishonouring those who have given their lives in the conflict, the inability to do justice for the dead, to hold them in memory and believe that their deaths were not in vain. These feelings, which could turn into violent action if not properly handled, are a recipe for the cycle of violence which begets more violence and loss of more lives. Examples of this specific route are found in most other conflict situations.

Thatcher-Gorbachev Learning Curve

David Markay (2009, p.16)[14] notes how two politically opposed arch rivals in the persons of Margaret Thatcher and Mikhail Gorbachev managed to find their own paths to reconciliation. In the middle of East-West political tension of the 1980's the two cold war ideological warriors met for the first time in Thatcher's residence at Chequers in the December of 1984. When she was asked in a subsequent interview what her impressions of the Kremlin leader were, she gave her now famous response "we can do business together". Markay says, "no gushing compliments, no tearful renunciations of past policies, no warm hugs. In fact, she continued by saying, 'we both believe in our own political systems.... he firmly believes in his; I firmly believe in mine, we are never going to change one another.'" Nevertheless, there was the possibility that they could do business (2009, p.16). There is a moral in the 'Maggie-Gorbie' learning route, to contain all conflict situations without simplifying any of the contemporary conflict contexts which includes the Israel-Palestine debacle too.

Radical Gospel Formula

If such was a response of two largely diametrically opposed political camps symbolized by the Thatcher-Gorbachev discourse, then how much more a Christian approach could and should portray towards other conflicts and other bitterly divided communities. The Christian claim is the embrace of the other, even the offender, and it remains the fundamental obligation of Christians who worship the God of unconditional and indiscriminate love. This radicalism is socially significant and is what gives credibility to the Jesus formula of pushing the defined boundary in order to re-carve frontiers of adjusting identities and self-understanding. This repositioning of the Christian approach is the beginning of the search for a truth that frees both the victim and the perpetrator. Justice does not dawn from heaven without human involvement; neither is it given on a platter by someone whom the parties think as powerful. The search for justice is imperative not just by one party, but by both camps, as justice might have been denied to both. This denial of justice in various layers in different times in each of their histories in fact might be the very reason for the conflict which perhaps in the present crisis is not even discussed or on the agenda for resolution. Hence, forgiveness and reconciliation is very much part of the Christian response to justice. The offending party and the offended party are natural to a conflict, but in fact both parties might have been offended and offending to each other too. Hence both need to embrace the most difficult aspects of the disbursement of justice in forgiveness and reconciliation. This does mean that provision for reparation must be in place instead of retribution, seeking restorative justice even within a punitive justice system.

The greatest contradiction is when believers quarrel with each other for so called 'God's interests' and do not realise that they fail by 'God's logic' so desperately. However, it is also important to understand that despite them being believers, yet they will still quarrel for things they fail to share, care and bear. They exhibit their own religious symbols on roof tops, yet they destroy the other's symbols because they disagree on language, territory, race, tribe, caste, colour and ethnicity. They feel ashamed, but pride hides shame. Attempts to claim supremacy, precedence and primacy over the 'other', make this 'other' a potential or actual enemy, while trying to promote something superior of the 'self'. Hence the narrative of the God of unconditional love who reconciles human activity without condoning injustice, alongside its desired formative traits in the lives of individuals and their communities, is the radical core of the Gospel. This is a challenge emerging in the same narrative manifesting to the three religious cousins. Those engaged are then allowed to reconstruct a political behaviour at all levels, but more importantly in political governance, particularly among majority-minority societies. Such societies are in fact increasingly the largest in the global context.

Victim-Perpetrator Antinomy

The contemporary Israel-Palestine conflict echoes and recasts the related symbolism, metaphors and partisan truth-claims of the three faiths to the extremity of the very denial of the existence of the other[15]. Both public pronouncements and other political mobilisations have historically managed to secure their own ardent supporters, sympathisers and a global portrayal of each side as a victim of the perpetration and the perpetuation of terror and violence by the other party. This territorial conflict, driven by historico-political rivalry and fuelled by ethno-religious feelings led each party to settle down as an innocent victim of an accusing perpetrator out there. This sustained belief has been profusely supported by distant actors in other global communities, and has further blinded each party to their own perpetrating and perpetuating hatred, terror and violence towards each of their communities.

However, it is in this context, for the remaining cousin of the family of Abrahamic tradition, that the Christians are compelled to reflect where they would fit, and what they can contribute firstly to understand the conflict in its geo-political context. Secondly, they could be part of the improved formula to search for a solution and thirdly they could ascertain theologically how their religious faith and their inspirational text, the Bible, could make sense of the mess of this conflict, which seems to have no light at the end of the tunnel.

What apparently emerges out of the conflict is a politically charged victim-perpetrator dichotomy. It is relayed that one camp and its sympathizers name the other as the perpetrator when actually both camps have been in a vicious cycle of being both the perpetrator and the victim at different times of the conflict. It is a fact that religious texts have been mobilized and reduced to a simplified commentary on contemporary events. They have been selectively read[16] and understood with little or no connection with the religious feelings of the people and the history of this patch of land in the conflict. What is more un-theological is that such reading of texts has also bypassed the pain, the loss and the apparent socio-political and economic disparities, power manoeuvring and the historical motifs of the situation in order to sacralise the conflict itself [17].

Cain and Abel story highlights an awakening and a responsibility

The perpetrator-victim notion in the biblical tradition appears early in the book of Genesis. The story may be interpreted in such a way that difference is integral to creation and without difference creation seems incomplete and unmanageable. Abel's sacrifice is different from Cain's as character traits are different too, even though Yahweh delights in Abel's. In God, difference is elevated as reconciliation, which is God's nature. Freedom is granted to the domain of human action. This difference between the two brothers indicates the awakened freedom of action on the part of humans, but reminds them of the moral and social responsibility towards the other, who is different and also as unique as oneself. The superiority of oneself does not come in power that one exerts, but in the ability to relate insightfully to 'difference' even when it appears intolerable. The conversation between Yahweh and Cain[18] summarises and opens several universally valid moral and ethical underpinnings of what helps wholesome human conduct in the world of difference. The inexplicable difference people face is a challenge to each community on how responsibly they behave towards each other. Cain's premeditated murder of his brother Abel may have been seen as a 'perfect elimination of difference'. His disagreement and non-compliance with his brother's difference makes him a man void of his own identity, as it is the difference in Abel that enhanced Cain's individuality and self worth. Cain's refusal to accept the difference of the other (Abel) as a positive element and a blessing brought damnation to one who is separated from the wholesome way of being. Hence the murder of his brother Abel made him not just a perpetrator but the victim of his own allegiance and alliance with evil. He neither listens to the external warnings of Yahweh prior to the act nor to inner promptings, but allows violence to prey upon him. He succumbs to evil, forming a 'victim character of the perpetrator'.

Khalil Gibran reiterates this human burden in his usual mystical words and phrases which might further illustrate the need for an awakened spirit and a governing responsibility for human action.

> "And this also, though the word lie heavy upon your hearts:
> The murdered is not accountable for his own murder
> And the robbed is not blameless in being robbed.
> The righteous is not innocent of the deeds of the wicked.
> And the white-handed is not clean in the doings of the felon.
> Yea, the guilty is oftentimes the victim of the injured.
> And still more often the condemned is the burden bearer for the guiltless and unblamed." (Gibran 1992, p.56)

Neither the victim nor the perpetrator is guiltless or blameless. Sympathy can be drawn for both parties, but it does not mean that one party is righteous by any means, according to Gibran. Hence his suggestion "you cannot separate just from the unjust and good from the wicked" (1992, p.56), seems like a roadmap for reconciliation in which both parties be brought to sense of reality. This sense of reality is not devoid of the place of God and the belief in that God of the parties, in this case the Israelis and Palestinians, who say and vouch that they are firmly anchored in the Holy texts and the guidance of Adonai/Allah.

'Many-ness' versus 'Same-ness'

However, what both groups have conveniently bypassed or left unsaid are the many unbearable scars of damage to families, the lies and untruths, and that what stands amidst them is shamefully irreparable. More cogently, what is clear is the complete abandonment of both groups of God's horizon as reconciliation and each group's inability to reconcile with God. As in the prototype story of Cain and Abel to which they both relate, they act in condemnation and vilification and have opted to fight 'God's interest' at the expense of each 'other's right for survival'. Reconciliation within God's proposition encourages human effort to pursue justice, and this justice is justice to both the innocent and the guilty, because they are only declared either innocent or guilty in the presence of God, as each party in theological terms accepts the primacy of God's rule in their pursuit for justice.

However, the biblical story of two brothers is more than just an illustration of Yahweh's agenda for reconciliation. Instead, it proposes a practical answer for Christians and others, that God's boundary expands the human standards of behaviour and conduct. Neither Cain nor Abel is the solution in God's thought process in the context of the story. Hence, partisanship either for Cain or Abel by the on-lookers would not help in the final resolution to their own situation. While the story denounces the despicable murder of an innocent, the project to wipe out 'many-ness' from human activity to create 'same-ness' fails, as Yahweh's justice must prevail. Yahweh is the author of the 'many-ness' of the creation, and cannot be nullified by human craft and avenging behavior.

A Moral Burden

The story of two brothers is not simply about murder or evil alone, instead it is about Yahweh's formula for reconciliation which embraces and ennobles difference with a new dignity that is life saving and not enslaving. The saving paradigm of the universal approach of God/Allah/Adonai was always expressed through a particular formula. Perhaps, according to Jonathan Sacks, "In the course of history, God has spoken to mankind in many languages: through Judaism to Jews, Christianity to Christians, Islam to Muslims. Only such a God is truly transcendental – greater not only than the natural universe but also than the spiritual universe articulated in any single faith, any specific language of human sensibility." (Sacks 2002, p.55) He daringly ratifies how God acts too in many ways to express Godself, challenging the human pride, greed and hatred which emasculate the very God-given gifts of reconciliation, forgiveness and the will to move forward gracefully. God's universal action shared by Jews, Christians and Muslims in the primordial story is a profound invitation to move on. Sacks is poignant in his insight when he argues what could work towards reconciliation in real life, "God *is God of all humanity, but no single faith is or should be the faith of all humanity. Only such a narrative would lead us to see the presence of God in people of other faiths. Only such a worldview could reconcile the particularity of cultures with the universality of the human condition*." (2002, p.55) The Cain-Abel narrative indicates the universality of a human condition in the premeditated act of Cain against his brother Abel. The demonisation of the weak, isolating the innocent and taking over their lives, unilaterally deciding their present and future with no reference to any other agent is a terror led conflict. Such acts then become what Gibran calls a "burden bearing of the guiltless and the unblamed" (1992, p.56), hence the moral burden invariably demands reconciliation even when one party triumphs as victorious.

Recycling Goodness

Life in the Yahweh paradigm neither ends with murder of the other nor with damnation of the perpetrator as both indicate negativity recycling the darker aspects of life: death and condemnation. Yahweh as Lord of life and hope requires fullness of life which is an invitation to restore and not destroy life. This gift reaches its highest point in the response of accepting the others as distinct persons in their created difference, as it contains dignity, beauty, vibrancy and the potential to celebrate it. Christian pedagogy in the person and the praxis of Jesus is no monopoly of the innocent. The self sacrificing act of reconciliation depicted on the cross is not a symbol of antagonism, spite or revenge. The cross opens a new possibility for reconciliation between enemies to resolve enmity and rise above mutual cruelty. For Christians, a place for redeeming axiom lies neither with Cain nor Abel, as it does not create any boundary on compassion, forgiveness and ultimate reconciliation, a gift on offer. The preferential option for the truly believing community in the Israel-Palestine conflict is neither pro-Israel nor pro-Palestine but for the solution to the menace of human cruelty to fellow human beings.

Scripture can be transformative as well as hegemonic in the wrong hands. It can be salvific as well as 'te(rror)xts'[19] instigating quite the opposite of what it really means to readers. It offers alternative positive readings for the context and the approach of visualising the 'other' in one's own 'camp'. All scriptures promote the values of justice, peace, reconciliation, and forgiveness – impulses of God's Reign, hence cannot take 'God's interests' in one's 'own logic'.

Three Cousins yet to relate to one another

All theologies whether they be Jewish, Christian or Islamic would be enriched by ongoing dialogue with the realities of the situation in Israel-Palestine and would inform such theologies to expand their horizons to see beyond the home front for a trustworthy insight and to recognize with hospitality the ending hostility. Independently politicized theologies connected to the prolonged agony can only be terminated when parties recognize the futility of the continuous burden of history.

The Serbs and Croats lived nearly 50 years under Marshal Tito. They became friends and neighbours, and their old hatred seemed to have remained dormant. The shift of power structure within the Balkans made friends into enemies. Neighbours turned historical antagonists. The retaliations in this part of the world were not second to any other conflict zones in other parts of the world. Such recreated antagonisms have been further accentuated by newly learned methods of inflicting maximum damage through arson and other means of destruction to fellow human beings, property and public assets. Undefined violence takes to the streets with mob psychology aggravating the situation on the ground to uncontrollable heights, anarchy taking power over all aspects of decency and rational behavior. The Israel-Palestine conflict is no exception to this pattern of violence-led behaviour. The tragic example of such conduct was the 2009 January spree of violence in Gaza where a whole people seemed to become an object of blame, even though the damage and the level of atrocities committed cannot be described as collateral by any means. Such levels of unmitigated acts of violence have in fact derailed the already fragile lines of communication. Two years on, nothing substantially has surfaced even though the Obama administration did take a keen interest in providing a different kind of diplomatic push-pull intervention with its allies among Middle East peace makers and other international bodies.

It's an act of faith by the Abrahamic Faiths

Rabbi Sacks, once again with his in-depth knowledge of Hebrew Scriptures, makes an attempt to recapture its meaning to the contemporary reader. He says that, "the world of the first eleven chapters of Genesis[20] is global, a monoculture.... It is to this world that God first speaks. He gives Adam a command, Cain a warning, Noah His grace. Yet, one by one these experiments fail. Adam disobeys, Cain becomes a murderer, and Noah inhabits a world filled with violence." (2002, p.51) 'The Lord regrets', Sacks says, for "He had made man on earth and His heart was filled with pain." [xxi] However, Genesis moves very quickly to bring back the authorship of God as One who is willing to negotiate with humanity. The moral here is, if God, who is believed by Jews, Christians and Muslims as the creator and the sustainer of all of them, is willing to make provision despite the failed experiment, then it is imperative that the three cousins need to make negotiations ceaselessly, even if peace is yet to be achieved. This Abrahamic scriptural admonition can scarcely be abandoned by any serious respondent from within these three faiths. However, the stalling journey towards a negotiated settlement for this troubled land is no easy yoke to carry for those who have been hurt and have agonised for a very long time. What hinders a possible solution at present is partly the burden of history and human pride culminating in greed for dominance instead of a keenness for healthy governance of a territory and the affairs of its people who are Jews, Christians and Muslims. Christians from within the context of Israel-Palestine, who also have their own relationship with Jews and Muslims historically, could engage as co-pilgrims in international deliberations and in theological reflection.

The solution for the Israel-Palestine conflict is being attempted and may be drafted via the roadmap for peace as suggested, with the two state solution as it is popularly known, which seems to have attracted many involved in peace negotiations even though there are logistical differences. This however does not mean that the hardliners, within the conflicting parties, and, perhaps more significantly, within the global support base for both parties, are amenable even to the two states solution which according some political commentators is part of a procrastination of a lasting solution. However, whatever finally becomes the positive direction towards a solution must be presented as a pilgrimage where the participants act as co-pilgrims, in order to whet the religious aspirations of the three Abrahamic faiths. They need to reflect and discern together, never in isolation, but acting in association, with a sense of hope and direction for a future unknown within the present economic crisis but whose destiny can be determined by paying attention to one another and working together for mutual survival.

The Israel-Palestine issue is not just a political question, but deeply a historico-religious antinomy with several road blocks of agony and pain, betrayal and being forgotten. They are 'Religious Cousins' at loggerheads now with less shame but sharpened with pride and obsessed with a history that is painful, burdensome and seemingly irredeemable.

The revered Abrahamic faiths of millions today have a civic and a global responsibility to make the process work by their informed and measured response to the tarnished and perhaps undisciplined reservoir of information that is sometimes unhelpful to a considered resolution of one of the world's most complex, calcified and longest conflicts. Building trustworthy relationships which will allow change and transformation can come about through continued dialogue and constructive confrontation in the spirit of Christian affirmation of life and order, amenable to interreligious conversations, without which Christian theology may find it hard to make sense of its own viability in the equation. If Christians cannot be a bridge by their own historical uneasiness and other circumstances, yet they could make themselves available as flexible conduits generating transparent engagement no longer as appendices, but as trustworthy partners towards a settlement. A sense, not of a Christendom concept that is bygone, but a renewed Christ-centred stewardship for a cordially coded agreement to live in peace in the Middle East, the land of many shared histories for these three faiths.

Epilogue

Religious traditions divorced from the daily realities of their adherents may possibly be considered faithful to scripture, but may not be true to the longings of the people who suffer pain, hunger and loss. If religion is an accomplice to this conflict, then it has lost its very purpose of being a beacon of light in times of darkness and apathy. Religious traditions, in this case the three

Abrahamic cousins, came historically alive during the time of each of the socio-cultural decadence or upheaval of their contexts, reviving with new hope, gathering their aspirations as a people. Moses brought together a people from slavery to freedom giving them dignity and hope. Jesus recaptured the heart of the faith of his ancestors, and rejuvenated that with his understanding and the realisation that God as Abba-father and the reign of God belongs to all. Mohammed in the Arabian peninsula managed to organise the aimless nomadic Bedouins and gave them a code of conduct to live by, which he received from Allah through the mediation of an Angel. These three spiritual men profoundly speak about an experience of the Divine in the human terrain. Their followers have lived through the test of time, following each of their key beliefs and energising hundreds of thousands of people. Now it is in their hands to show whether they in return can be faithful to what they assertively observe is a transformative way of believing and belonging. If this aspect of their faith is undermined, then new generations would neither be interested in believing nor in belonging to any of them.

The Israel-Palestine conflict is so well known and notorious as a human failure with all the current skills of diplomacy and other international tracks of strategic planning for governance and the deployment of democracy. In fact this conflict is so ingrained, that Israel has almost become synonymous with Palestine and vice-versa. If the word 'Palestine' is mentioned, people in a listening audience would expect Israel to be mentioned. All who participate and listen in the same audience would obviously be divided on this subject, and the feelings of solidarity with one or other side rise automatically: such is the implication of this conflict in an average public discourse around this subject. Some have given up on it and moved on to different areas with their separate deliberations, yet not without drawing a party line, while others would robustly try to confront the same burden of a past that they possibly cannot carry.

The Israel-Palestine conflict is not a global conflict but a globally connected geo-political stalemate. Therefore a globally supported resolution must be attempted even though such a solution need not be fully agreed by all sympathisers. The Northern Ireland peace package and its final show-casing is still fragile, yet it taught certain lessons for all peace negotiators across the world: the need for new ways for acceptable governance, mutual trust, co-responsibility, the acute need for transparency and accountability by the leadership. It indicated that parties in conflict are not all, as Gibran says, 'white-handed is not clean,' because there is no 'guiltless or unblamed' in a conflict. But what is unacceptable is that all the blame is on one side and that all goodness is on the other side.

There is no perfect righteousness in any conflict, but righteousness is at the core of the solution – the most difficult journey, as tough as the actual conflict itself. Peace making is a visionary task, and requires an abundance of graceful approaches by men and women, to energise them to alleviate their burden of history, pain and ill feelings towards the other, and elevate such to a new level of thorough and mature meeting of the enemy as human beings and equals, but honestly acknowledging that all have wronged each other. The Victim-Perpetrator language must be abandoned in a definitive way, even though its residual influences may linger and may surface in both formal and informal conversations with the respective parties.

Religion, faith and their well founded, well sourced scripture, well argued and well formulated doctrines still may sound like profound impediments for a negotiated settlement. But such doctrines must be accepted as a genuine and authentic background to each of their identities and which makes them what they are as a people. The difficulties and shortcomings will tend to derail such conversations as they are part of the main agenda. But they must never be bypassed without being addressed. Each party must be confronted with the challenge that, in the event of a derailment of their agreed peace formula, new waves of suffering and agony for their own people would be set off. Recognition of the conflicting parties as agents of change and not the culprits of history is an immensely enabling status that must be proudly bestowed upon the parties to the conflict. Even though the notion of a perpetrator-victim has been cyclically part of their histories, it can no longer be entertained in view of the hope for peace which is now to be harvested. Their precious history, religious, cultural and other forms of being who they are, must be part of each amicable, acceptable and negotiable step towards a solution which can be provisional until parties feel comfortable. Such progress in the Israel-Palestine conflict should be possible and would be a glimmer of hope. Some of it is already in place as projected in the recent Kairos Palestine Document[xxii] produced in the style of the famous South African Kairos document[xxiii].

The religion of all parties has been interpreted in ways to create a definite and a permanent enemy, and has been part of the problem over the years. If religion were to be part of the solution, then it would rise above its critics to save itself to be a catalyst of transformation, a champion of justice and mover of people and become the change itself.

---

[3] They were an ethnic Tamil militant group that fought a secessionist battle against the majority Sri Lankan Sinhala dominated governments over nearly three decades. They were finally defeated in May 2009 seemingly by a well coordinated military offensive by the Government of Sri Lanka, amidst highly vocalised opposition by the Tamil Diaspora in most global Capital cities of the world. There were also known as Liberation Tigers of Tamil Eelam (LTTE).

[4] His first was *The Age of Revolution 1789-1848* (1962) second, *The*

Age of Capital 1848-1875 (1975) and third, *The Age of Empire 1875 - 1914* (1987). His latest is *The Age of Extremes 1914- 1991* (1995)

[5] It is my view that most conflicts lingering today have some geopolitical implications in what I identify as 'three historical endings' and 'a beginning' – End of World War II, End of Colonialism, End of Cold War and the 'Beginning of War on Terror'. These also have direct links to most contemporary conflicts. Perhaps Hobsbwam in his next exploration might survey 1991- 2009; 'An Age of Globalism' is my suggestion for him.

[6] The neo-liberal market agenda found its bedfellows in the policies of both Ronald Reagan and Margaret Thatcher in their approach to economics, politics and international relations. This apparent triumph declared that it would be a new world order. In 1992 the US based Japanese American Francis Fukuyama produced *The End of History and the Last Man* which gave a basis for why the liberal democracy might be the solution for the world's problems.

[7] The Diaspora mobilisation during the height of the Sri Lankan Government's offensive on the Tamil Tigers (March–May 2009) was very prominent to the extent of disrupting the daily routine of urban life in the global Capitals. It is also further observed how the same Diaspora has been able to mobilise the masses to conduct referenda in the post war era in many European Tamil Diasporas and Canada for an establishment of a separatist Tamil State in the North and East of Sri Lanka.

[8] The political dissension between the HAMAS (*arakat al-Muq wamat al-Isl miyyah*, meaning 'Islamic Resistance Movement') and FATAH (*arakat al-ta r r al-wa an al-filas n* , meaning the 'Palestinian National Liberation Movement'. From this was crafted the reverse acronym *Fat* (or *Fatah*), meaning 'opening', 'conquering', or 'victory') within the Palestinians. It was called among Palestinians *Wakseh,* meaning humiliation, ruin, and collapse as a result of self-inflicted damage (Conflict of Brothers). The internal political bickering in Israel between the ultra-orthodox Zionists and other Jewish leaders sympathetic to the 'Two State Solution' has made the self inflicted wound to the Jewish community at large.

[9] It is the obvious enmity through a series of 'over reactions', and 'betrayals', an inability to keep to the negotiations agreed upon by both parties, suicide attacks and disproportionate military offensives and the calcification of these matters without a reasonable break which adds to the primary conflict. Also this is one single conflict that has a 'worldwide partisanship', sometimes not even properly informed about the historical nature of the conflict. I have found that some individuals right across continents have opted to support either party, for no reason other than its popular appeal. To react is a psychosocial need for human beings to make their identity affirmed and re-rooted with the oppressed or the oppressor.

[10] A term popularly used to describe a time in Western philosophy and cultural life, centred upon the eighteenth century, in which reason was advocated as the primary source and legitimacy for authority instead of other religious or political authorities. Some are of the view that the religious resurgence of the later part of the twentieth century into the new Millennium is a socio-cultural reaction to these reason-based thought patterns that seemed to have consciously marginalised the religious and their scriptural authority, which dominated Western thought for centuries up until the eighteenth century.

[11] Reading of the Bible differs in unimaginable ways since the time of the reformation. Biblical studies in fact have become a specific and highly specialised hermeneutics of understanding the sacred scriptures and their 'Sitz im Leben' (place in life). However, Christians are divided among themselves as to how they wish to read the same text. This diversity has also promoted a diversity of approaches, understanding and development of ideas while it has also brought new rivalry among Christians on many fronts. This includes the possible solution to the Israel-Palestine issue.

[12] Following the birth of political Zionism in 1897 and the Balfour Declaration, the League of Nations granted the United Kingdom the British Mandate of Palestine after World War I, "...such political, administrative and economic conditions as will secure the establishment of the Jewish national home, as laid down in the

preamble, and the development of self-governing institutions, and also for safeguarding the civil and religious rights of all the inhabitants of Palestine, irrespective of race and religion" See Article 2, *The Palestine Mandate of the League of Nation*, 24 July 1922. Sighted http//www.medeastweb.org/mandate.htm. 11 Sept. 2010. It is be mentioned here that in November 1947 the United Nations decided on partition of Palestine into a Jewish state, an Arab state, and a UN-administered Jerusalem.

[13] Land of Israel (*Eretz Yisrael*), a concept central to Judaism since biblical times and the heartland of the ancient kingdoms of Israel and Judah. Over the past three thousand years, the name "Israel" has meant in common and religious usage both the Land of Israel and the entire Jewish nation. According to the Bible, Jacob was supposed to have renamed Israel after successfully wrestling with an angel of God – see Gen. 31:24-32. Christians similarly have expanded the concept of "Israel" in their own liturgies, especially in the use of the Psalms, where Israel has become the code word for the Church or the Reign of God.

[14] He is a pastor at a Multicultural Methodist Congregation in Milan. See "A Parable" (2009). Also visit www.corrymeela.org

[15] *Both the late president of Egypt Abdul Gamal Nasser and the President of Iran publicly denied Israel's right to exist. Even though Israel has not declared itself in such an identical way, it has acted in terms of the occupation and acquisition of land since the Belfour declaration in 1917. However, the US born Rabbi Meir Kahane founded* **Kahane** *Chai in early 1970's and initiated the Kach party. The two were marginal extremist Israeli groups that have used terror to pursue their goals of expanding Jewish rule across the West Bank and expelling the Palestinians. They were Israeli militant groups that advocated the expulsion of Arabs from the biblical lands of Israel. Kach, as well as the Kahane Chai, condones violence as a viable method for establishing a religiously homogenous state.* See ***http://www.cfr.org/publication/9178/*** sighted on 22.10.09

[16] These specific readings of texts are hugely problematic as it contravenes the Universal appeal of the particular sacred literature and narrows it down to a tribal interpretation which then loses both

its sublime calling and what it stands for: the sake of the human family. Sacred scripture can only be transformative for the user and never should become a guide for destruction.

[17] The Military Rabbinate, a unit in existence since Israel's foundation, has been headed by the 57-year-old Brigadier General Avichai Rontzki for the past three years. A fellow traveller of Rontzki, Shlomo Aviner is one of the head ideologists of the militant settlers' movement. Aviner teaches that the Land of Israel belongs solely to the Israeli people, is holy and may not be contaminated, for example by"autonomy" – clearly referring to the Palestinian issue See.http://www.qantara.de/webcom/show_article.php/_c-476/_nr-1153/_p-1/i.html, sighted on 25.10.09

[18] See Genesis 4:1-16, especially vv 9-16

[19] This particular word was improvised by Dr. Sathi Nathan Clark at a private seminar when he was talking on 'Religious Fundamentalism' and made reference to the dangers of indulging textual literalism by various religious groups, St. Philip's Centre, Leicester, 19 Oct. 2009.

[20] The first book of the Hebrew Bible is a revered text by all three Abrahamic faiths. Especially the range of characters that appear in this section reappear in their own respective sacred texts and are considered as important personages each in terms of their history.

[21] Genesis 6:6 also see Sacks (2002) for further interpretations of Genesis verses.

[22] The Kairos Palestine Document: A moment of truth: A word of faith, hope and love from the heart of Palestinian suffering, co-authored by over a dozen Palestinian church leaders and theologians from various denominations, and the result of an 18 month-drafting process, document date: 11.12.2009. See entire text

http://www.oikoumene.org/gr/resources/documents/other-ecumenical-bodies/kairos-palestine-document.html, sighted 30.12.09

[23] It is known as The Kairos Document (KD) since it was the first of its kind. It was a theological statement issued in 1985 by a group of black South African theologians based predominantly in Soweto, South Africa (however there were also white South Africans involved in the formation of the watershed document). The statement

challenged the churches' response to what the authors saw as the vicious policies of the Apartheid state under the State of Emergency declared on 21 July 1985. The names of the authors were never publicised at the time. KD became a breath of fresh air to the frontline churches and other activists around the world to gather momentum to end a regime that the document itself considered 'sinful'.

Jerusalem in Imagination and Reality

Mark Chapman

'Jerusalem' in Popular Imagination

In April 2011, the Duke and Duchess of Cambridge chose William Blake's 'Jerusalem' as one of the hymns at their wedding at Westminster Abbey, which was watched by many millions of people across the world. Parry's stirring tune seemed to fit the occasion well. The hymn does not seem to have provoked any controversy, which has not always been the case. In 2008, for instance, the late Dean of Southwark, Colin Slee, is reported to have banned the singing of 'Jerusalem' at a private memorial service in his cathedral. A spokesperson commented: 'The Dean of Southwark does not believe that it is to the glory of God and it is not therefore used in private memorial services.'[1] Seven years earlier a bride cancelled her wedding in Cheadle when the Director of Music and the rector objected to the singing of the song. They regarded it as 'too nationalistic'.[2] 'I enjoy it as a mystical poem,' the rector commented, 'but it is not a prayer and it is not about God. Nor is it addressed to God, and nor does it contain any of the themes you would expect of God'. He is also reported as saying that

> "people tended to interpret the poem in the nationalistic sense that England is best. ... What most people actually want is Hubert Parry's tune, so we sometimes suggest other hymns

> to the same music. Indeed, Martyn [the Director of Music] has himself written a hymn on marriage and God's love to the tune of Jerusalem."

Victoria Williams, the bride, was exasperated by the decision: 'I could not believe it,' she remarked. Similarly, her father described the ban as

> "disgusting. ... Victoria has liked Jerusalem since she was a child and watched it on television being sung at the Last Night of the Proms. She really wanted it at her wedding. It was, after all, her big day – not the rector's. The whole family is upset."

While I would not wish to comment on the pastoral sensitivity of these decisions, nor on whether or not the clergy involved were justified, what I think is important is the passion which singing a two stanza poem about Jerusalem can arouse.

It is perhaps rather surprising and even strange that people in England should sing a patriotic song about a city in Asia Minor, which had for a long time been administered as part of the Ottoman Empire, and which, at least when the words were written, very few people had ever seen. And even when Sir Hubert Parry wrote his stirring tune during the First World War, Jerusalem was a city populated mainly by Muslim and Christian Arabs with a small Jewish quarter. What I want to reflect on in this paper is the Jerusalem of the imagination and the real Jerusalem, and, most crucially, on the relationship between the two, which is not always as straightforward as it might seem. In recent years, with Christian pilgrimage becoming far more commonplace because of much easier communication, it is not clear that the Jerusalem and the Holy Land that are visited by pilgrims have much to do with the politically and religiously divided city of the contemporary world. The religious imagination of the pilgrim can obscure the contemporary realities of place.

This is obviously not just a modern problem. Jerusalem has always been a city which speaks powerfully of the connection between vision and reality. This is principally because this relationship itself is at the heart of the Christian story: the vision of a Kingdom is always tempered by a social and political context. Thus, shortly before he died, Jesus is reported to have wept over the city of Jerusalem (Luke 19:41-44); but soon afterwards that very same city had been transformed into the heavenly city of the Book of Revelation (especially chapter 21). By the nineteenth century, when William Blake (1757–1827) composed his strange lines, Jerusalem had become a vision of a better England. The heavenly Jerusalem thus reveals itself in a variety of different contexts. As an illustration of the relationship between vision and reality the reception history of Blake's poem is particularly illuminating.[3] Indeed, the power of a poem to evoke a passionate response in several different contexts, especially when combined with music, displays something of the potency of the imagination as it inter-relates with a whole range of complex realities.

The poem that is sung as the hymn was part of the preface to William Blake's epic poem, 'Milton', written in 1804 during the Napoleonic wars but not published until 1810-11. The preface and the poem were a consciously prophetic piece. The 'Jerusalem' poem was immediately followed by the Biblical text: 'Would to God that all God's people were prophets' (Numbers 11:29). The prose preface that precedes the poem similarly illustrates Blake's prophetic intentions and the redemptive power of art:

"Rouze up O Young Men of the New Age! set your foreheads against the ignorant Hirelings! For we have Hirelings in the Camp, the Court, & the University: who would if they could, for ever depress Mental & prolong Corporeal War. Painters! on you I call! Sculptors! Architects! Suffer not the fashionable Fools to depress your powers by the prices they pretend to give for contemptible works or the expensive advertising boasts that they make of such works; believe Christ & his Apostles that there is a Class of Men whose whole delight is in Destroying. We do not want either Greek or Roman Models if we are but just & true to our own Imaginations, those Worlds of Eternity in which we shall live for ever; in Jesus our Lord." (Erdman 1981, pp.95-6)

As this passage shows, Blake was a man with an extraordinary and lively imagination.[4] In the 'Jerusalem' poem in the preface to Milton, Blake draws on the strange legend that Joseph of Arimathea, who was supposedly a tin merchant, had brought the infant Jesus to Glastonbury. While the legend is far-fetched, it nevertheless inspired Blake's imagination. The poem also includes the imagery of the Chariot of Fire which took Elijah to heaven (2 Kings 2:11). For Blake, the horrors of industrialism were signs of the corruption of Reason. The dark satanic mill of the poem may well have been the giant Albion flour mill on Blackfriars Road, one of the first factories in London. In what might have seemed a portent, the mill had burnt to the ground in 1791 – his vision in the poem was of a different sort of society built on the genius of poetry and art which would supplant the earthly city.

This short poem in the preface to Milton, however, was not Blake's only poem about Jerusalem, which remained a persistent theme in his writings. His epic poem 'Jerusalem', published in 1804 (in Erdman 1981, pp.144-258), is extraordinarily complex in its imagery, much of which blends scenes from London with scenes from the Old Testament. A short distinct passage reflects similar sentiments to the 'Jerusalem' poem from the preface to Milton:

"England! awake! awake! awake!
Jerusalem thy Sister calls!
Why wilt thou sleep the sleep of death

And close her from thy ancient walls?

Thy hills and valleys felt her feet
Gently upon their bosoms move:
Thy gates beheld sweet Zion's ways:
Then was a time of joy and love.

And now the time returns again:
Our souls exult, and London's towers
Receive the Lamb of God to dwell
In England's green and pleasant bowers." (Erdman 1981, p.233)

Taking on the mantle of the prophet, Blake campaigned against rationalists such as Newton and Locke through an odd amalgam of mysticism and religion expressed in writings and drawings. Far from being an orthodox Christian, he was deeply influenced by the occult and the Swedenborgians. His literary and artistic work is not surprisingly full of bizarre and sometimes apocalyptic imagery, which at times is scarcely comprehensible.

So how is it that a peculiar piece of visionary poetry, so disliked by the rector of Cheadle and dean of Southwark, became what *The Times* once called almost a 'second national anthem'? The story is an interesting one and points to the complex relationship between the ideal and the real, to keeping alive a vision of hope in the reality of the world. It would seem that Blake's poem was not at all well known until the end of the nineteenth century. It was almost certainly because of the idiosyncratic clergyman, Stewart Headlam (1847–1924) that Blake's poem became better known – and through him it came to be associated with the Christian socialist cause.[5] For his time, Headlam was a very unusual character: he never really had a parochial job, having had his licence revoked in 1883 for his support of abolition of the House of Lords, but instead became an unofficial chaplain to the ballet, music halls and theatres, which in those days were highly suspect places. He also stood bail for Oscar Wilde during his trial. He is most famous, however, for forming a small group of radical socialist clergy called the Guild of St Matthew which he led from 1877 to 1909. In 1884 Headlam bought a journal called the *Church Reformer* which he made into the mouthpiece for his ideas. He quoted part of Blake's poem in bold print under its masthead, using the passage from 'I will not cease from mental fight' to the end (Orens 2003, pp.54-5). From this point on 'Jerusalem' seems to have been associated with radical ideas.

The idea of putting music to the poem came a little later on – it was the brainchild of Robert Bridges (1844–1930), the poet laureate during the First World War, and a prolific hymnodist. Bridges, who had been a friend of Sir Hubert Parry (1848–1918) since their schooldays at Eton, had suggested that the composer might write a tune for a gathering of an organisation called 'Fight for Right' that was holding a rally on 28 March 1916 in the Queen's Hall in London. The Fight for Right Movement had been set up in September 1915 to promote a continuation of the war, its object being 'to assist in rousing men and women to enthusiastic service in the fight for ordinary human rights against the staggering blow which Germany is dealing to them'. Although it supported the war, its aims were not simply jingoistic. Instead it was an organisation that sought to promote a more universal vision of humanity: 'right will only win through the purification of the efforts and sacrifices of men and women working not only for their country but for the whole of humanity'.[6] The movement had been set up by the explorer and pioneer of inter-faith relations, Sir Francis Younghusband (1863–1942), and attracted speakers of a more reflective character than many other rallies at the time. Justice rather than victory at all costs was at the heart of its language.

Sir Henry Newbolt, who spoke at one of the early lectures, claimed that the allied forces should be fighting for an ideal rather than simply for a finite goal. The slogan was 'Fight for the Right till Right is Won'. This had even been set to music by Ernest Austin (1874-1947) and after it had been sung by Geoffrey Gwyther, the audience joined in repetition: music was thus an important part of the Fight for Right Movement from the beginning. Although *The Times* reported that the 'the words are not remarkable; the tune is not a masterpiece', it nevertheless claimed that there was an 'inspiration which comes because there is a big idea behind the mechanism of expression': this put it in a higher class than 'the hundreds of topical songs that are pouring from the press'.[7] Whether such a mediocre song inspired the search for something more fitting for such a noble idea is unknown, but Edward Elgar, England's leading composer, was approached to compose a special 'Fight for Right' song. He set some words of William Morris (Kennedy 1968, p.293; Banfield 1989, vol 1 p.137),[8] which were sung for the first time at a meeting of the Movement on 21 March at the Queen's Hall by the well-known tenor, Gervase Elwes, and dedicated to Members of the Fight for Right Movement. This meeting was addressed by William Temple, at the time Rector of St James's, Piccadilly and Millicent Fawcett (1847–1929), the leading suffragist and feminist.

Early in 1916 Robert Bridges suggested to Parry that the setting of 'Jerusalem' for the 28 March 1916 rally, which would have a large choir available, should be 'suitable, simple music to Blake's stanzas – music that an audience could take up and join in'.[9] Bridges also suggested that if he was not able to undertake the composition himself he might delegate the task to the composer George Butterworth, who was away fighting at the front at the time, and who was killed later in 1916 (Graves 1926, vol. 2 p.92).[10] In the event Parry undertook the commission and wrote down the music on 10 March. Parry's pupil, Henry Walford

Davies (1869–1941), organist at the Temple Church (and soon to become first musical director for the Royal Air Force), commented later that Parry had shown him the manuscript at the Royal College of Music on the 'memorable morning'[11] of the following day. Walford Davies and Parry had been active in promoting performances of music in the Music in Wartime Movement (Colles 1942, p.106). Reporting later on this meeting Walford Davies commented that Parry had given him the score with the words: 'Here's a song for you. Do whatever you like with it'. He took it away to secure publication and copyright for Parry (Colles 1942, p.107). Eleven years later, he looked back on the event:

> "I recall vividly his unwonted happiness over it. ... He ceased to speak, and put his finger on the note D in the second stanza where the words "O Clouds unfold" break the rhythm. I do not think any word passed about it, yet he made it perfectly clear that this was the one note and one moment of the song which he treasured. ... We needed it for the men at the time ... I know Dr Bridges specifically wanted every one of us to sing it, and this is happily coming true."[12]

At the Fight for Right Meeting Robert Bridges gave the opening address. Other speakers included the Belgian advocate, M. de Leval, who had tried to save Edith Cavell, and Evelyn Underhill, the Anglican writer on spirituality.[13] In its report of the meeting, *The Times* called Parry's melody one of 'inspiring breadth'. It had been sung by 300 volunteer voices 'belonging to the chief choral societies and choirs of London' conducted by Walford Davies, who infused the performance with 'vital energy'. Other music performed included Purcell's 'Soul of the World', and Parry's *Voces Clamantium*. Harold Darke's 'The Reveille', sung by the male voices, 'roused the audience to such enthusiasm that it had to be repeated'. Elgar's 'Fight for Right' song was also sung by John

Adams, and Walford Davies had set Shakespeare's 'O England, model to thy inward greatness' from Henry V.[14]

It did not take long for Parry's 'Jerusalem' to become associated with the Fight for Right Movement. In a report of a patriotic choral competition held on 3 June 1916, *The Times* referred to 'Jerusalem' as Parry's 'noble "Fight for Right" song'. It continued: 'Here was courage and order at its highest power'.[15] The association of 'Jerusalem' with Fight for Right displays again the problem of connecting the vision with the reality: during an appalling war a group of relatively liberal-minded people sought to keep a vision alive of a just peace, and a sense of universality beyond narrow nationalism. Despite the inevitable compromises, Blake's words expressed a hope for a universal and peaceable kingdom, of something far beyond the terrors of war or the narrowness of jingoism. Even so, Parry was far from being a wholehearted supporter of the Movement: he accepted the commission primarily because he was a friend of Bridges. In August 1916 he refused to set Paul Loyson's 'Pour un chiffon de papier' for another Fight for Right rally (Dibble 1992, p.484).

The Fight for Right Movement continued through 1917, organising public meetings and lectures.[16] But it eventually folded at the end of the year as its cause had been taken up more generally by the National War Aims Committee.[17] Nevertheless the popularity of the Fight for Right song continued, although it had migrated into another field altogether – its continued success depended on Millicent Fawcett, who was President of the National Union of Women's Suffrage Societies (Rubinstein, 1991). The Representation of the People Bill had passed through parliament with a large majority early in 1918, and a celebratory meeting was held afterwards at the Queen's Hall on 13 March (Rubinstein 1991, pp. 241-2; Graves 1926, vol 2, pp.92-3). By all accounts this was an impressive gathering – Mrs Fawcett had even managed to persuade Parry, who died only a few months later, to conduct the

London Symphony Orchestra and 'full choir' (made up of members of the Bach Choir) in a new orchestral setting of Jerusalem. Parry himself had supported the cause (Graves 1926, vol 2, p.146), and his wife, Maude, was a prominent suffragist. Fawcett, who later recollected that the poem had been set specially for the Women's Movement (Fawcett 1924, pp.250-1),[18] wrote to Parry straight after the performance:

> "The music said for us what no words could say, and it was an added delight that you were in charge of it all ... The Council passed a special vote of thanks to you, the Bach Choir, and the Orchestra yesterday, but this is a little personal line. Your Jerusalem ought to be made the Women Voter's [sic] Hymn." (Graves 1926, vol 2, p.92)

Parry certainly appreciated the invitation, writing in his diary:

> Lively uproar of joy when Mrs Fawcett went on platform. She spoke with sense & humour ...The music went very well. The sound of "Jerusalem" when the audience joined in was tremendous.[19]

From that date the song became associated with the women's movement, and was soon adopted by the Women's Institute as its anthem.[20]

The most famous setting of 'Jerusalem' was the lavish orchestration by Sir Edward Elgar composed in 1922 for a large orchestra at the Leeds Festival: it continues to be a feature of the Last Night of the Proms. Upon hearing this version for the first time, King George V said that he preferred 'Jerusalem' over the rather more dreary God Save the King. In 1927 *The Times*, reviewing a centenary exhibition about William Blake, wrote the following about the hymn:

> "It has become almost a second National Anthem – nay, if it be not disloyal to say so, it has come to stand for something that the National Anthem fails to express … "Jerusalem", in fact, has become the hymn for those special occasions, on which the private Englishman … finds the need for expression, impossible in his own words."

Apparently without much sense of irony *The Times* could see a poem about a city in the Middle East as a suitable national hymn for England: it was capable of expressing 'the private loyalty to some Little England'. The city, which in 1927 was populated mainly by Arabs and under British control, was identified with 'the white and secret Albion of Blake's imagination'.[21] Rather more dispassionately, Stephen Banfield sums up the popularity of 'Jerusalem' in comparison to other patriotic songs:

> "[Jerusalem] more than any other song except 'Land of Hope and Glory' since 'Rule, Britannia,' has become part of the national heritage, but whereas 'Land of Hope and Glory' is, for all its inspired melodiousness, a four-square tune with maudlin words fitted to it, 'Jerusalem' is a model of subtle phrasing, finely sculpted declamation and melody free of clichés – principles which Parry pioneered and which have distinguished English solo song in its finest periods. For such a refined tune to have become so popular is surely unique. Its success must have brightened what little was left of Parry's old age." (Banfield 1989, pp.137-8)

Jerusalem combines an extraordinary combination of words and music which undoubtedly rouses the emotions, but at the same time it invites the singer to share in Blake's vision of a better England. Indeed the early history of Parry's setting reveals the power of the creative imagination, but also the different realities to which Jerusalem was related: from Blake to Headlam, from Bridges to Fawcett, there were quite distinct contexts with which Jerusalem was connected.

Imagining the Holy Land

The above discussion of the history of a popular hymn illustrates something of the complexity of the relationships between vision and reality. Jerusalem could function in very different contexts as a way of reaffirming a vision of a better world, yet one always mediated through particular contexts. The importance of the ideas of Jerusalem and the Holy Land in the popular imagination should not be underestimated. The very language of the 'Holy Land' implies a universalism of place in which all Christians have some sort of stake. Christian language at all levels continues to be shaped by the meanings that are attached to particular places. This again says something about the strange clash at the centre of the Christian life: the clash of the real and the ideal; between vision and reality. In the Christian tradition, of which Blake's poem is just one example, Jerusalem becomes a symbol of hope – a vision of heaven, but at the same time it is always inevitably a real place inhabited by real people. This is as true in our own time as it was in Jesus's time. There are two sides to the Christian story – and the theological task is to weave them together in the contemporary world which is neither simply the old Palestine nor the New Jerusalem.[22]

When thinking about Jerusalem a key problem is of how the vision of the heavenly makes contact with the earthly. This is an obvious implication of the incarnation where God is made manifest in Palestine at a particular point in time in the person of Jesus Christ, fully human and fully divine. Indeed, it is inevitable that Christianity, as a religion based on the particular history of Jesus of Nazareth, should place special weight on the historical places of his birth, ministry, and death. However, even though

Jerusalem is and always was a real place, it is also at one and the same time the spiritual destination of all those who practise the Christian religion: it functions as a symbol for the coming reign of God. This blend of the historical with the eschatological remains true today: the cities of the Holy Land are simultaneously places of longing in the religious imagination of contemporary Christians, as well as real towns inhabited by real people in what is now the divided country of Israel/Palestine. The ease of travel and the popularity of pilgrimage make this tension very acute.

This is not, however, a new problem. The relationship between the ideal and real in English conceptions of the Holy Land has been well charted by Eitan Bar-Josef in his fascinating account of the Holy Land in nineteenth-century English culture (Bar-Josef, 2005). From a variety of perspectives he describes the English perception of Jerusalem and Palestine before the collapse of the Ottoman Empire and the Balfour Declaration, and just how extraordinarily Anglicized it often became. A good example comes from Henry Hart Milman, who wrote his controversial book on the *History of the Jews* in 1829. He provoked the wrath of some in the church by having the audacity to describe Abraham as 'the sheikh or emir of a pastoral tribe, migrating from place to place. ... He is in no respect superior to his age or country, excepting in the sublime purity of his religion' (1850, vol 1, p.28). For Milman, Abraham looked something like the contemporary Arab: it was as if Palestine was a kind of living museum of Biblical times; and as if its inhabitants had not really changed at all.

Others who went to the Holy Land could not even begin to understand it except in terms of their very English conception of Christianity. What was crucial about visiting the Holy Land, claimed A. P. Stanley, Dean of Westminster, was the feeling which it should awaken 'in the hearts of thousands far away in England'. According to Stanley, a visit to Palestine would reveal the true meaning of what it was to be English. In fact, he claimed, what was important was not the present-day Holy Land, but 'the heavenly Jerusalem, which is the mother of us all'. At the same time, however, he remarked in a letter that the scenery was very homely, and rather like the rich valleys of Derbyshire and Yorkshire but with olives.[23]

In the late nineteenth century there were many efforts at trying to create a more accurate mental picture of the Holy Land. To this end there were a number of extraordinary travelling exhibitions where entrepreneurs and missionary societies took over church halls, covered the floor with sand, set up a few Middle Eastern artefacts and employed the local population to act as Palestinian natives. The 'Palestine in London' Exhibition from 11 June to 2 July 1907, for instance, attracted over 350,000 visitors to the Islington Agricultural Hall. The guide book claimed that 'the visitor should be able to learn more in a day than he could otherwise learn by an actual visit in an entire week' (Schorr, 1907, p.19; cited in Looker 2002, p.26). Similarly, at the World's Fair in St Louis in 1904, eleven acres were devoted to a reconstruction of Jerusalem. (Bar-Josef 2005, p.154). On this sort of perception of the Holy Land, it was quite obvious that a twentieth century Arab was much the same as a patriarch of 2000 BCE, or, for that matter, a shepherd from the nativity story.[xlv] The orientalism of such events was scarcely appreciated at the time. For instance, *The Times* could write about the 1886 Colonial and Indian Exhibition: 'the visitor is carried from the wild, mad, whirl of the individual struggle for existence to which civilisation has been reduced in the ever changing west, into the stately splendour of the unchanging antique life of the east'.[24]

As these examples demonstrate, Jerusalem and the Holy Land conjure up so many images which are based not on contemporary reality but on a huge range of mythical representations in art and poetry. For Christians, the 'Holy Land' has never been approached 'neutrally', but is a place whose landscape has already been visited in the imagination, and which features in the mental pictures of the scenery and topography of the Gospels and the Hebrew Bible. Undoubtedly for many in the nineteenth century, Palestine belonged to all Christians. It is therefore no surprise that William Thomson, Archbishop of York could claim at the Annual Meeting of the Palestine Exploration Fund in 1875 that

> "our object is to know Palestine through and through, to work with every one who will assist us; and our reason for turning to Palestine is that Palestine is our country. I have used that expression before, and I refuse to adopt any other. That is my country, which has given me the laws by which I try to live – which has given me the best knowledge I possess – that is my country, to which I look for rules in the conduct of my life—in which has dwelt my King and my Lord. England is my country, I know it and feel it, but Palestine also is my country. I am sure you all know and feel as I do, and that is the reason you take such an interest in the quiet work of this excellent Society. (Cheers.)"[25]

What emerges from this discussion is that, even at a time when archaeological exploration of the biblical sites was beginning in earnest, there was still the constant temptation to blend the real with the ideal: Palestine belonged to everybody rather than simply to those who happened to live there and who held the deeds to the land. On the one hand, there was the vision of an ideal Jerusalem and Holy Land which was based on a need to be at home in the Christian religion: this meant that Palestine might be like Yorkshire, or, for those whose visions were wilder, it might be something more apocalyptic like Blake's prophetic use of Jerusalem, or it might perhaps be a more Orientalist picture of an uncivilised country, a kind of living museum inhabited by noble savages. On the other hand, however, there was always that real land with its cities and towns.

It is not clear to me that much has really changed: the perception of the Holy Land is perhaps still coloured by the visions and longings of past generations. However, where Blake's vision is obviously something imagined and a product of the fancy, which is always prophetically contrasted with the realities of his context, the other visions of the Holy Land in the nineteenth century, and which in many ways continue to flourish today, are far less obviously the dreams of a lively mind. Yet there is a sense in which those who visit the Holy Land experience it as they want it to be, or at least as how the tour leader wants it to be. And this experience may well be a long way removed from the realities of the Holy Land today with its conflicts, markets, shops, restaurants, churches, mosques, synagogues, and people. Today, of course, it is a land where there are internal borders, checkpoints and an impregnable wall between Israel and the area administered by the Palestinian Authority (although much of it is built on Palestinian land). But for many pilgrims it may well continue to be every bit as much like Yorkshire as it was for Dean Stanley, and the rustic shepherds may appear to be no different from those who inhabited the land in Abraham's time.

Pilgrimage

This clash between the ideal and real versions of the Holy Land provides the backdrop for discussing Israel and Palestine in the context of pilgrimage. For many British Christians familiarity with contemporary Israel/Palestine emerges from the experience and theology of pilgrimage: while most Christians will not have visited for themselves, many will know people who have been on pilgrimage or organised tours to the religious sites of the Holy Land. A great deal of the experience will obviously depend on the particular religious or political ideology of the pilgrimage organisers and tour guides: given the preconceptions of the Holy Land which, as I have suggested, exist among all Christians – and which are made significantly more complex in the post-1948 and 1967 and more recent settlements – it is crucial to reflect on the nature, purpose and significance of pilgrimage, especially as it relates to the 'real' life of the contemporary Holy Land. Pilgrimage – like the concept of the Holy City itself – reflects something of the clash between ideal and real.

While it is impossible to go into any detail, it is obvious from a cursory reading of church history that pilgrimage is a complex phenomenon. This is equally true for the theology of pilgrimage. On the one hand, in its most idealised form, pilgrimage is characteristic of the Christian life in general: it depends on the logic of discipleship, of following Christ into the unknown but towards the heavenly city. This understanding is emphasised, for instance, by the concept of the 'resident alien', which has been developed in recent years by Stanley Hauerwas, among others.[26] This idea is rooted in the notion of the Christian as a 'stranger and exile' (Heb. 11.13) or as a citizen of a commonwealth which is not of this world (Phil. 3.20): for the Christian, as for the Son of Man, there is nowhere to lay one's head (Luke 9:58). On this model, there is an inherent restlessness in the Christian journey of discipleship, which makes it impossible to stand still in the world. John Bunyan's *Pilgrim's Progress*, which stresses the idea that pilgrimage is identical to the Christian life, rather than a temporary visit to some holy place, is perhaps the archetypal protestant allegory of the Christian understanding of pilgrimage as the journey of life. The idea of life as a pilgrimage, however, is certainly not restricted to Protestantism: as was emphasised at the second Vatican Council, the Roman Catholic Church regarded itself as the eschatological community of the 'pilgrim church'.[27] In turn, in the church's earthly liturgy 'by way of foretaste, we share in that heavenly liturgy which is celebrated in the Holy City of Jerusalem toward which we journey as pilgrims, and in which Christ is sitting at the right hand of God, a minister of the sanctuary and of the true tabernacle of God'.[1] While this is obviously a spiritualisation of the earthly city of Jerusalem, the city is nevertheless mentioned by name as the destination of the Christian life (as in Rev. 21.2). This understanding of pilgrimage is the stuff of visions and eschatology: and it is to Jerusalem that everything is orientated.

On the other hand, however, from the very beginnings of Christianity, pilgrimage has also referred to the process of journeying towards specific and tangible holy places. Almost from the beginnings of Christianity, there was an emphasis on visiting the Holy Land, venerating those places associated with Jesus Christ, as well as the Old and New Testament: grottos and rocks commemorating events in the life of Christ were acknowledged from very early on in the history of the Church. Constantine's mother, Helena, for instance, made her famous journey to the Holy Land from 325-7 in search of relics and in order to establish pilgrimage churches at the holy sites. Towards the end of the fourth century (c. 381-4) the pilgrim Egeria travelled, probably from Spain, to Egypt and Palestine to experience for herself the places mentioned in the Bible, and to share in the ceremonies and liturgies that had developed in the pilgrim sites. At about the same time a number of women, including Jerome's friend Paula and her daughter, Eustochium, established a hospice for pilgrims visiting Helena's Church of the Nativity in Bethlehem. The Franciscans were given custody of the sites and were responsible for hospitality from 1384. Despite the religious and political turmoil of the following centuries through Ottoman rule, pilgrimage remained. And obviously in an age of mass travel, when even EasyJet flies to Tel Aviv, pilgrimage continues unabated even through times of conflict.

What seems important in any contemporary theology of pilgrimage is that it should embrace both the ideal and the real: like the rest of the Christian life, pilgrimage will be inspired by a vision of a better world, a New Jerusalem, and it will be focused on the attempt by the Christian to understand more of the implications of discipleship, both corporate and individual: the eschatological dimension cannot be ignored. At the same time, however, pilgrimage will remain little more than visiting a 'living museum' unless it locates the pilgrimage in the complex social and political reality of the present. For Christians, it seems to me, this is the implication of the historicity of the incarnation: the Christian religion began at a particular time and place, and it is lived out today in particular places and times. Visiting the sites of Christ's ministry in order to walk where he once walked is at the same time an act of re-imagining the past and the future in the reality of the present.

This means that a pilgrimage which takes the incarnation seriously – as distinct from simple tourism – will be both a religious experience and at the same time an experience of contemporary life in the place of pilgrimage: vision and reality should be combined. It is impossible, for instance, to visit the Sea of Galilee without observing the Golan Heights; similarly, it is not possible to visit Bethlehem on the old pilgrimage route from Jerusalem without passing through a checkpoint. Guides sometimes have to be ingenious in order to avoid this and to accompany their groups and to stay in the city. Nazareth is the scene of inter-religious conflict stemming from the attempt to build a mosque which would have obscured the basilica of the Annunciation: the belligerent posters are obvious to any visitor. A visit to Bethany, which is increasingly rare on pilgrimage itineraries, means seeing an isolated town with the security wall constructed across the main street, and where the inhabitants are increasingly isolated from the outside world. The differently coloured number plates will be obvious to anybody travelling on roads in the West Bank.

Conclusion

The theological basis for the sort of pilgrimage which takes the lives of contemporary people seriously, and which sees them all as created in the image of God, rests on the historicity of the Christian religion, which is lived out in the real conditions of the present in remembrance of the past for the sake of the future. This means that the pilgrimage itself embraces something of the past and future but also becomes a forum for discussion of Israel and Palestine in the present. While there may be a remembrance of the Jerusalem of the Bible, and a longing for the prophetic New Jerusalem, the Jerusalem of the present simply cannot be ignored: as the example of singing about the New Jerusalem in the bloody conflict of the First World War illustrated, there is a complex relationship between vision and reality in any set of circumstances. It is not clear to me, however, whether most pilgrimages rise to this level: there often seems to be little awareness or questioning of the ideological presuppositions of the pilgrimage company nor of the social and political context of the contemporary Holy Land.

Nevertheless, it is possible that a theologically-rooted pilgrimage can provide an opportunity for 'deep listening': the voices of other people can be heard in an atmosphere of hospitality, and they can be brought into dialogue with the Christian vision of a New Jerusalem and in remembrance of the past conflicts in which the life and ministry of Jesus were located. While pilgrimage will not solve any of the intractable conflicts of Israel and Palestine, it nevertheless raises the need for education and discussion between different parties to the level of a religious duty. Conversation is rooted in the doctrine of incarnation: the ideal and the real co-exist in the act of remembering in the present for the sake of the future. The act of imagining the new and the old Jerusalem in the Jerusalem of the present is consequently inseparably connected to the reality of the hopes and dreams of those who live in the Holy Land today. And this brings with it a prophetic dimension of which William Blake might have been proud.

---

[1] *Daily Telegraph*, 9 April 2008.

[2] *Daily Telegraph*, 9 August 2001.

[3] Brief overviews of the history of the hymn can be found in Reeves and Worsley (2001) pp. 136-9; and Dearmer (1933) pp. 239-41. As far as I am aware the first hymn book to include 'Jerusalem' was Percy Dearmer's influential but highly eclectic collection, *Songs of Praise* (1925).

[4] On Blake, see Ackroyd (1995).

[5] See Orens (2003) pp. 239-41.

[6] *The Times* 14 September 1915.

[7] *The Times* 13 November 1915. Newbolt's address was later published, together with a selection of essays and lectures by other members of the movement in *For the Right: Essays and Addresses by Members of the "Fight for Right" Movement* (1918) pp.6-22.

[8] Elgar set a passage from 'The Story of Sigurd the Volsung and the Fall of the Niblungs' (1876).

[9] Bridges to Parry, no date (early 1916), cited in Graves (1926) vol 2, p.92.

[10] See also Dibble (1992) p.483.

[11] *The Times* 27 August 1927.

[12] *The Times* 27 August 1927.

[13] *The Times* 29 March 1916.

[14] This song is not listed among his published works.

[15] *The Times* 5 June 1916.

[16] Six meetings were held at the Aeolian Hall from 4 November to 9 December (*The Times*, 3 November 1917). They were preceded by an organ recital by George Thalben Ball.

[17] *The Times* 11 December 1917.

[18] Dearmer's account relies on this source (1933 p. 240). The error was pointed out in a letter to *The Times* by Herbert Hams on 20 August 1927.

[19] Parry diary, 13 March 1918, cited in Rubinstein (1991) p. 242.

[20] On this, see Gibson (2006). She is inaccurate in her dating of the writing of Parry's setting.

[21] *The Times*, 12 August 1927, p. 11.

[22] On something of the complexities of this task, see Ateek (2008), ch. 11.

[23] Citations in Bar-Josef (2005), ch. 2. See Stanley (1856), p. 102.

[24] A provocative and challenging discussion of orientalism in relation to conceptions of the Jesus of history in the context of international relations was made by James G. Crossley (2008), esp. ch. 6.

[25] *The Times*, 22 May 1886, p. 5.

[26] *Quarterly Meeting of the Palestine Exploration Fund* (London: Bentley, 1875), p. 115. See also Bar-Josef (2005) p. 92.

[27] See, for instance, Hauerwas and Willimon (1989).

[28] *Lumen Gentium* ch 7, §48 in Abbott and Gallagher (eds) (1966), pp. 78-85.

[29] *Constitution on the Sacred Liturgy* I.8 in Albert and Gallagher (eds) (1966) p. 141

Conflict and Religion

Douglas Hedley

"There is no document of civilisation which is not also a document of barbarism." Walter Benjamin (1950, p.258)

1. Religion, conflict and violence

I would like to start with a consideration of two books that appeared in 1972: the German Walter Burkert's *Homo Necans* and the Frenchman Rene Girard's *La Violence et Le sacré*. Burkert is an eminent classicist and Girard a literary theorist with a structuralist provenance. Both books present a gloomy anthropology preoccupied with violence. Both emerged out of the unprecedented scale of human suffering generated by two world wars, but both also drew on those reflections upon war and peace that extend from Homer to Tolstoy, Virgil to Shakespeare.

Burkert sees the violence of Greek myths and rituals as grounded in pre-historic hunter-gatherers. Homo sapiens was a hunter-gatherer for 95% of our evolutionary history and our relative recent history of pastoral civilisation bears witness to the submerged but innate instincts and deep memories of our violent hunting ancestors. Burkert sees this as the most satisfactory explanation for the widespread prevalence of bloody sacrifice in the ancient world. Burkert was deeply influenced by the Austrian Biologist Konrad Lorenz, who posits aggression alongside hunger, procreation and fear as basic instincts that we share with the rest of the animal kingdom. Greek legends and myths are very violent: one might think of the 10 year siege of Troy over Helen's abduction or Oedipus killing his father and marrying his mother!

Here we touch on ancient nature-nurture debates.

Girard also sees violence as a key to human culture. However, he is keen to emphasise the cultural mediation of elemental and ubiquitous human violence as 'mimetic desire'. This mimetic rivalry emerges out of the desire to imitate the imagined desires of other agents. This tendency to conflict and violence produces the need for a scapegoat. Girard maintains that the 'scapegoat mechanism' is the origin of human culture. Violence and the sacred are linked through the scapegoat: both the object of violence and yet revered as the condition of stability and the release from intolerable social collapse. Girard famously presents Christianity as unveiling and denouncing both these mechanisms: mimetic rivalry and the victimisation of a scapegoat.

Both Burkert and Girard are much debated and highly controversial figures. I think there are serious problems with both theories. However, they both present a powerful corrective to any jejune optimism about the human condition. Certainly it casts doubt upon the view of human beings as quasi-mechanical rational optimisers, e.g. rational choice theory. In particular, the view that sees religion as the main cause of violence looks implausible through the work of both men. Religion, for good or bad (largely bad for both the German and the Frenchman) is an attempt to address violence and conflict.

The problems in the 'holy land' constitute a clear instance of the close link between violence and the sacred. In this sense it seems to be a reversion to religious wars of the kind that seemed to be dwindling in significance within an increasingly secular world.

2. The imaginary
Ancient and primordial images suffuse the modern mind, whether it is aware of these or not (Mali, 1992). Though contemporary culture tends to diminish the significance of the historical, one

philosopher in the modern period who resolutely challenged this a-historical dimension of modern thought, and who identified it with the legacy of Descartes, was Giambatista Vico (1668-1744). One must consider the role of Vico in challenging the idea of a knowledge that comprises clear and distinct ideas, *l'esprit de geometrie*. Vico's critique of Cartesianism requires a strong philosophical theory of tradition. Vico's view of history is dominated by the concept of the 'ricorsi', the cycles of history, the view of history that we tend to associate with (disreputable) historians like Spengler and Toynbee. But the salient point is made by Vico. Through the idea of *ricorsi*, we can see Vico interpreting historical events through poetic archetypes, and to see the facts of history as part of an intelligible structure:

> "The poetic speech which our poetic logic has helped us to understand continued for a long time into the historical period, much as great and rapid rivers continue far into the sea keeping sweet the waters borne on by the force of their flow." (Vico 1999, p.163)

For Vico, the understanding of agency in the present must involve an awareness of the continuing significance of the past. Donald Phillip Verene has laid great emphasis upon imagination in Vico, especially the idea of *universali fantastici* or imaginative universals (Verene 1981). Vico also uses the terms *caratteri poetici* and *generi fantastici*. These several formulations of the same idea constitute a key element in Vico's thought: how human beings create society and thereby move from the stage of beasts to men. It is, for Vico, through imagination that we can appreciate how we can understand even the most alien of societies. Hence amid the apparently 'deplorable obscurity' of the ancient nations, we can find intelligible patterns. Among the very muddle of history, we can find materials for metaphysics. From the vantage point of a perspective like that of Vico, we can turn to reflect upon the impact of the 'imaginary' upon actions and events in history. Take, for example the impact of 'atheism' upon human history. The first great high point of atheism in modern culture was the French Revolution, a development deeply influenced and shaped by philosophical ideas. Indeed we might consider not just the atheism of the French Revolution but its other related ideas. 1789 is a nodal point for Occidental culture since the ideas of the French Enlightenment were put into practice in French and much of Europe in the wake of the Revolutionary wars. Many of the conflicts about religion in particular in contemporary states can be traced back to ideas of the French Revolution and the establishment of secular state in France. The French Revolution inaugurated a battle within our culture that has endured since, concerning the role of religion with public life. Europe is divided between those cultures that have retained the monarchy and an established form of Christianity like Great Britain or the Netherlands or Scandinavia (with the recent exception of Sweden) and secular states like France. Paradoxes abound here. The United States, notwithstanding its strict division of Church and State, is more evidently religious than 'religious' states like Britain or Norway. This can lead to practical problems, in particular the idea that the only the secular state can guarantee rights and liberties. The question of the Muslim veils is a typical example. In an explicitly 'secular' state freedom is the freedom from religious tyranny and thus such public symbols are viewed as subversive. From another historical perspective, e.g. in a country like the U.S.A, where freedom was often perceived as precisely the freedom to practice one's religion, actions such as the ban on the scarf seem draconian.

The great sterile beauty of Versailles became a mausoleum of the grandeur and futility of Ancien Regime, yet it exerted a symbolic power. Napoleon and the Bourbons refused to return there. After the collapse of the second French Empire and the capture of Louis Napoleon, King Wilhelm I of Prussia was declared Emperor of Germany in the Hall of Mirrors in the Palace of Versailles. This makes no sense apart from the German sense of humiliation throughout the 17th century and the Prussian revenge for that perceived servitude under the French domination.

3. The 'double bind' of Orestes.

It is a common failure to see ethics in purely economic terms as the weighing up of utilities. However, ethical problems sometimes concern *prima facie* incommensurable values, e.g. liberty and security, or equality and liberty. Orestes, the eponymous hero of the great drama of Aeschylus' tragedy, is presented with a paradigmatic conflict of values. Orestes for Aeschylus (unlike for Homer) is caught in a terrible conflict. His father Agamemnon has been brutally murdered by his wife Clytemnestra, the mother of Orestes. Orestes feels polluted by his deed and is pursued by the Furies. He seeks refuge with Apollo in Delphi and is then acquitted by Athena in Athens after trial by jury. The cycle of revenge is broken and a judicial system is founded. It represents the shift from bloody appeasing sacrifice: Iphigenia is sacrificed by Agamemnon to the order approved by the Gods, especially the 'all-seeing Zeus'. Aeschylus' play mirrors the shift from monarchy to democracy: the acropolis changes from being the seat of the monarch to the home of the gods, especially Athena. Law and democracy are replaced tyranny and vendetta. Aeschylus wrote the *Oresteia* in 456 BC and in 431 the Peloponnesian war began – with disastrous consequences for Athens.

The interests of the Israelis and the Palestinians are prima facie incommensurable. The Palestinians understandably view the Israelis as rapacious invaders and conquerors, cynically supported by vast alien power in the U.S. The Palestinians cannot be expected to view the ghettos, pogroms and concentration camps of Europeans as sufficient reason for the expulsion of Palestinians from their historic land. The Israelis view the Palestinians as stoking the latent anti-Jewish sentiment of the Arab world and harbouring terrorism, and as an abiding threat to the idea of existence of the state of Israel.

4. Wars and Terrorism?

Israel/Palestine has been the site of wars and terrorism since the British Mandate. Ought implies can: responsibility presupposes freedom. Killing or injuring another human being is obviously wrong and yet most societies suspend this in the case of war and punishment. Let us take war to be military conflict between political bodies. I assume that both pacifism and militarism are implausible positions: war cannot be avoided and yet it is always an evil. Pacificism cannot cope with the first fact and militarism denies the latter. I assume that war is a necessary evil, one that should be strenuously avoided (Guthrie and Quinlan, 2007).

The Israel-Palestinian conflict seems a typical instance of the kind of conflict of interests that ensues in violence. Clausewitz said that 'all war presupposes human weakness and against that it is directed' (1937, p.257). Israel is surrounded by apparently hostile states. On the other hand it is supported by the U.S., and is widely perceived as a U.S. satellite.

There is problem with the asymmetry between the Israelis and the Palestinians, in at least three senses. Firstly, because the Palestinians, Muslim and Christian, have no state. Secondly, one might consider the rapid transformation in the territory of Palestinians since 1948. Israel constitutes 78% of the land of historic Palestine, which prior to 1948 was largely Arab. The Palestinians seek to have a small state upon the remaining 22% of the land (West Bank, Gaza and east Jerusalem). Even this remaining territory land is divided up through settlements and Israeli roads and checkpoints.

In the terminology of just war theory, *jus in bello*, this seems to infringe both principles of discrimination and proportionality. The first bars the deliberate attack of the innocent. The second is where incidental or collateral harm outweighs any military benefit. Even if the first is rejected, it is hard to avoid the conclusion that the Israeli attacks on Gaza lacked proportionality. There has been widespread concern in recent time regarding the plight of Palestinian civilians in Gaza.

Gaza, it has been noted, resembles a jail. But Israel, despite it military prowess, is itself trapped in a prison of fear and instability: retaliation and the erosion of law. The indiscriminate violence of the Hamas rockets and the ensuing anxiety generates more walls and blockades: literally and figuratively. Israel needs security and peace with its neighbours in order to flourish. Unless the Palestinians are forcibly removed – like the Canaanites – the Israelis must find a way of negotiating with Palestinians. The security and flourishing of both are indissoluble.

The fanaticism of the extremists on both sides is a development that is closely related to the modern ideal of a single ethnic-religious definition of the land. Such an ideal is completely at odds with the history of the land itself in the pre-modern period.

The position of Palestinian Christians seems most poignant. The Christian West largely ignores them and their existence complicates the politics of the Holy Land for those who wish to envisage or cynically present the troubles as essentially a conflict of Islam and Judaism.

5. Imagination, tradition and History: The Break up of Empire and the failure of the New Utopias

The 'holy land' – the sacred home for the Jews, despite the secular nature of the state of Israel, is a very powerful idea. In its recent history it emerges from a context of persecution and war and European nationalism.

The political order of the early modern period prior to the French Revolution was largely dynastic-sacred rather than national-secular. The Ottomans were not 'Turks'; the Prussian court spoke French during the age of Goethe; the Emperor of the Germans sat in Vienna or Prague. The Holy Roman Empire, neither Holy nor Roman perhaps, nevertheless expresses the residual feudal ideals of old European order. It was doubtless an imperfect order, but order it was. And it had great precedents: Alexander's Empire and Virgil's vision of the *Pax Augusta* or Dante's vision of a politically united Christendom in his *De Monarchia*.

The wars of religion in the 17th century created devastation in Europe. Writers like Grotius tried to develop an influential secular justification of the political order, one that moved from transcendental or sacerdotal reasons to issues of human need and justice. The Enlightenment in Europe was distinguished by this shift from the religious to secular legitimization. Grotius was a Christian, but he was motivated by the brutality and disruption of the European wars of religion (Howard, 2002).

One of the great ironies of the 20th century was that prominent 'secular' national totalitarian states were crueller than the Empires of the ancient regime. The slaughter, deportation and starvation, and rapacious conquest of millions under Stalin, Hitler and Mao would have astonished, perhaps even appalled, legendary tyrants like Tamburlaine, Genghis Khan or Attila. Visionary conservative thinkers like Burke (1790) and de Maistre (1797) predicted that modern Utopias would generate terrible tyranny. Burke and Maistre appealed to the terror of the French Revolution as a harbinger of future horrors and as a vindication of their conservatism.

I sympathise with both Burke and Maistre. The break up of old European and Ottoman order, the removal of these dynasties through Enlightenment ideas, revolution and war is often seen as the march of progress. Yet these old multi-ethnic, multi religious dynastic orders were often cultured and tolerant. Stalin and Hitler were typical of new ruthless, intelligent and resentful men from the provinces (Georgia and Upper Austria), both steeped in revolutionary ideas and ideals – embodying the will to power that despised and destroyed the decaying aristocratic milieu of Czars and the Kaiserreich. The Romanovs, Habsburgs or the Ottoman rulers created resentment and injustice but held together rich and diverse cultures – often with great success. The break up of these empires was instrumental for the Palestine/Israel question. Zionism and National Socialism grew out of the Habsburg twilight. In the wake of the defeat of the Ottoman Empire, Britain's promise to give the Jews a homeland and to liberate the Arabs generated the present problem in Palestine/Israel.

The German atrocities committed against European Jewry and the murder of 6 million Jews during the regime of NSDAP (National Socialist Party of the German Workers) are obviously part of the *ratio essendi* of the Jewish state. The cruel persecution of Jews under Stalin can only have reinforced the Zionist demand for a homeland. It is of note that we use a theological-sacrificial term for the 'Holocaust'. The official secular and Neo-Darwinian-socialist ideology of the NSDAP was that of a 'final solution' (Endlösung). That term had pragmatic or biological but no theological connotations. 'End' in German does not have the teleological connotations of English 'end' or French 'fin'.

In the second half of the twentieth century the Soviet Union and the United States were vigorous exponents of 'post-colonialism'. The disastrous American involvement in French Indochina and the Soviet invasion of Afghanistan may have looked like imperial adventures but the Americans and Soviets employed a very different justification. The militant atheism of the Soviets and the strict separation of Church and State in the U.S. meant that their 'empires' has no explicit religious ethos. Whereas Britons had fiercely protected Protestant settlers and Spaniards or Frenchmen had nourished Catholic colonies, the new powers had no explicit religious agenda.

The rise of the religious right in the US and radical Islam throughout the Muslim world changed the complexion of certain conflicts, especially after 9.11. Religion is not likely to disappear from the public domain in the Holy land. The eradication of religion per se, or the removal of competing religions, is clearly not the solution. Some *modus vivendi* for the flourishing three religions of the region is required. That presupposes work of reconciliation. And reconciliation requires both forgiveness and the establishment of justice. And I shall argue that these two should properly be understood and mutually reinforcing.

6. Forgiveness and Justice

In considering the concept of forgiveness, I shall turn to the great English philosopher – Bishop Joseph Butler, one of the towering intellects that the Church of England has furnished for European Philosophy. For Butler's classic analysis, forgiveness, resentment, revenge and the notion of shared humanity are the pivotal ideas (1726, Sermon VIII). Butler's thesis is that resentment is the precondition of forgiveness. He sees forgiveness as the 'foreswearing of revenge' but this presupposes a genuine resentment towards the agent who has inflicted the injury. The motive for forgiveness is the recognition of a common humanity. Butler dwells upon the command of Jesus to 'love thy enemy'. Rather akin to the spirit of Kant's distinction between practical and pathological love, Butler thinks that though an affection cannot be commanded, but rather one is required to view one's enemy as another human being and thus to recognise their frailty and imperfections.

Butler differentiates between anger and resentment. The former is 'hasty and sudden' anger whereas the latter is deliberate and sustained over times by one agent towards another. Anger has it classic expression in Homer's reference to the 'gall of anger that swarms like smoke inside a man's heart and becomes sweeter than the dripping of honey' (1924, 18:1-7-110). Butler further notes that resentment normally implies a moral estimation, one based on a sense of unfairness. Charles Griswold in his impressive book, *Forgiveness, A Philosophical Exploration* notes that the etymology of resentment (in the French re-sentir) supports Butler's distinction between the instantaneous emotion of anger and the sustained sentiment of resentment. The victim has not merely been harmed through some physical or mental damage, but wronged. Butler thinks that a further condition of forgiveness is the resentment felt by the victim towards the wrong doer. This is a natural and proper feeling. However, it can – if excessive – lead to revenge. Resentment is not inconsistent with goodwill, for we often see both together in very high degree not only in parents towards their children, but in cases of friendship and dependence where there is no natural relation. These contrary passions, though they may lessen, do not necessarily destroy each other. We may therefore love our enemy and yet have resentment against him for his injurious behaviour towards us. But when this resentment entirely destroys our natural benevolence towards him, it is excessive and becomes malice or revenge (Butler, 1726). Thus the victim of an injury may still harbour resentment towards an offender but these sentiments remain in proportion to the offence.

To err is human, to forgive divine. However, forgiveness should not be confused with becoming supine (Griswold, 2007, p.19). As Kant observed, if you make yourself a worm people will step on you (1996, pp.187-8). Does arbitrary forgiveness undermine morality? This claim is made by Celsus against Origen.[1] Forgiveness can seem close to condoning or forgetting a wrong. A recent philosopher Brudholm has argued forcefully that forgiveness is often irrationally preferred over resentment: 'the preservation of outrage or resentment and the refusal to forgive and reconcile can be the reflex expression of a moral protest and ambition that might be permissible and admirable as the posture of forgiveness rather than the first stage in the process of forgiveness (Brudholm 2008, p.4).

There are prudential reasons for forgiveness which do not seem very compelling ethically. However important it may be for one's psychic health to 'let go' of resentment towards someone by whom one has been injured, this does not seem to have much of a basis in morality in the strict sense. Hick's critique of Swinburne (Hicks 1994, pp. 247-264) depends upon a view of forgiveness which omits some of the complexity surrounding the concept. Ironically, Hick's God becomes a rather *arbitrary* being. Forgiveness cannot consist in the disregard for justice.

7. Punishment and Divine Goodness

The concept of forgiveness also shows the metaphysical inadequacy of naturalism in dealing with ethical questions. Could animals forgive? The answer is clearly no. The capacity to forgive presupposes a uniquely human (or Divine) responsibility and rationality. In the wake of so many theories of both 'religion' and 'altruism' that are grounded in evolutionary biology or cognitive science, forgiveness is an instance of a distinctly human space of reasons that are hard to reduce to considerations of adaptation and survival. Thus a full-blooded metaphysical account of forgiveness can be a welcome antidote to implausibly reductive accounts of interpersonal relations. Perhaps our general tendency to generate ill and wrongs is not a set of bizarre projections onto a bare and meaningless moral landscape but the infringement of an objective moral order.

If the rationale for punishment is not just Utilitarian principles like deterrence or prevention of crime, questions of justice and freedom, forgiveness or mercy cannot be arbitrary. It is the *conscious* and *free* act of the offender that makes punishment necessary. The closely related concepts of mercy and forgiveness need to be distinguished. Forgiveness is a mental state whereas mercy is an act. The former is a revision of one's attitudes or dispositions, whereas the latter is the mitigation of an otherwise merited punishment. To treat a person with mercy may involve giving him less than his just deserts. However, if the virtuous agent embodies justice and mercy, there must be some consistency. Mercy, Jeffrie Murphy claims, can be 'morally dangerous sentimentality' (2009, pp.168-9). Mercy requires a theory of retribution since utilitarianism or deterrence theories of punishment: Richard Swinburne claims: 'mercy can only be meritorious if retribution is right. Mercy goes beyond justice' (1989, p.99).

8. Christianity and the theology of substitution.

Christianity has unique resources for addressing the questions arising from human conflict with great depth and power, though not always in a manner satisfying to economists or scientists. Yet as Aeschylus makes clear in his great trilogy *The Oresteia*, we are dealing with mysteries of the human condition. We can hardly expect limpid solutions to opaque problems. We must appeal to analogy and symbols. Yet, as psychotherapy insists, the exploration, articulation and reflection upon images can liberate human beings.

Judaism and Islam have no theory of the Fall and no theory of substitutionary atonement. I will bracket the questions of the precise understanding of the Fall or penal substitution in the Reformed tradition, i.e. that the substitution is one of punishment. The freedom of the individual is always viewed as significantly limited (because of sin) and atonement requires Divine grace.

One should consider the anti-Utopian dimension of Christian (the 'Fallen world') and idea of Christ's willing dying as a substitute for human failing. (I am, of course, aware of different traditions in both Judaism and Islam. However, the Christian theory of redemption is quite distinct from Rabbinic Judaism since AD. 70, and evidently distinct from Muslim theology, cf. Islam's rejection of incarnation in the Koran.) It is interesting to speculate about the extent to which the differing theologies affect theories of justice, punishment and reconciliation.

9. Hope and Myth: Violence and Imagination

It is a common error to think that tragedy necessarily ends in disaster. The *Oresteia*, though not quite a happy ending, is nevertheless positive. It is, as much as Plato's Republic, an account of justice and a rejection of the cynical 'might is right' doctrine of Machiavelli, Hobbes or Nietzsche. The progress in Northern Ireland shows that in very intractable conflicts progress can be made. But that conflict is one of the last instances of the European wars of religion, conflicting loyalties to monarch and pope. The deep antagonism and suspicion between Protestants and Catholics, and between the British and Irish governments, has been much reduced and, to some extent, resolved.

The EU is I think another instance of successful conflict resolution. Germany and France were bitter enemies between Louis XIV and Hitler. The fate of Strasbourg reflected those conflicts. The deep peace and cooperation of France and Germany is a very great achievement of the last fifty years. War between them now is virtually unimaginable.

The 'imaginary' of the Israel Palestine conflict is quite different. The foreign policy of the US and the worsening situation in Afghanistan and Iraq, fears about Iran and Pakistan have deepened certain political fault lines. In the wake of the soi disant 'War on Terror', the divisions in the Arab world and the hardening of opinion among Israelis means that the immediate prospects for practical resolution look poor.

10. Peace and Order

Augustine defines peace as harmony and accord (City of God XIX, 13). This requires a well ordered peace. If agreement is based on transient commonalities, then conflict will erupt. A defective peace, even one which was accepted with concord, will not be sustainable. However important charity, benevolence and love are, *justice* is equally important as an organ of peace. The establishment of justice within a state is difficult, without it, the establishment of order borders on the impossible. Governments found peace and peace needs just laws for it preservation.

It has often been noted that war is not a relation between human beings but between states and Kant in particular argued that war is inevitable without a 'cosmo-political constitution', (1790, paragraph 59) something like United Nations. Hegel poured scorn upon Kant's optimism because he could not see any way of a League of Nations exercising sovereignty and arbitration between states is very complex.

The fragility of human peace can be observed in the fact that great events have trivial causes. Even the assassination of Archduke Franz Ferdinand was the main cause of the First World War; a momentous event – but it hardly seems proportionate to the calamity of the 'Great War'. The human heart is not only restless, but deeply conflicted. We owe much to the optimism Enlightenment ideas and ideals and the reforming zeal they helped inspire. But the European Enlightenment tended to overlook the genuine place of spiritual ideals in human flourishing and was often tied to a naïve conception of human perfectibility. Ignoring salient facts about human nature, especially its propensity to violence, is a recipe for increased violence not its cure. The concord and justice required for lasting peace are not a matter of recalibration through social or political engineering but of renewal of the heart. Only the vision of God can provide that.

---

[1] Origen, *Conta Celsum,* Chapter XV. Griswold (2007) emphasises the extent to which ancient ethicists use *syngnome* to refer to those instances of ignorance, force or emotions affecting negatively the behaviour of an ethical agent.

The Language of Politics and the Language of the Cross

Patrick Riordan SJ

Some people object to the public exhibition of the cross or crucifix.[1] It is argued that human rights are violated by such public display, or it is argued that respect for minorities or adherents of other religions are likely to be offended by the public display of distinctively Christian symbols.[2] Christians, for whom the cross is a constant and familiar presence, may be surprised or even shocked to experience this antipathy shown towards the cross. What is for them an image of solidarity with suffering humanity is for others a gruesome intrusion on their consciousness. For many it is an image of brutality with which they would rather not be confronted. Parents in particular often wish to shield their children from exposure to the horrors of human reality. Another reason for objecting to the cross is that it has frequently been used as a symbol of domination. There are many examples from history: Constantine's *in hoc signo vinces*, the cross borne by Crusaders, colonisers in Africa, the Americas and Asia, quite happy to conceal their domineering ambitions behind the evangelizing and missionary rhetoric. All these examples are reminders that the cross has often been used as a symbol of and justification for domination and exploitation. So Christians should not be surprised when people express antipathy towards this revered symbol.

The historical misuse of the symbol is doubtless a hindrance to a grasp of its proper meaning. Is it conceivable nonetheless that a positive meaning for the cross might be recovered in purely human terms, accessible to those who don't regard it with

Christian faith? I suggest that an understanding of the full meaning of the cross will include an insight into the very heart of politics in the proper sense with the consequence that key values for politics might be jeopardized by a banning of the cross from public display. In other words, I argue that the exclusion of the cross from the public arena is in danger of undermining distinctively human values which sustain that arena. Instead of seeing the cross simply as a symbol for one major world religion, is it conceivable that it might be regarded in non-religious terms as evoking a human value which might be recognized as such by anyone? Just as the smiling Buddha can evoke for all onlookers, Buddhist or non-Buddhist, a sense of tranquillity and contentment, so might not the cross be a reminder for all whether Christian or not of the fundamental attitude required for any political handling of conflict?

In what follows I argue that politics in the full sense is fostered and facilitated by the human reality which the cross invokes. I focus on the human reality and leave aside for the purposes of this paper what Christians profess in faith. I acknowledge that this approach risks domesticating the reality of the cross. It also runs the risk of occluding central theological truths for the sake of highlighting important human aspects of Christ's cross. In this paper I explain what is meant by politics; how it is to be understood as a distinctively human achievement in the face of conflict. Where politics is achieved, it is precarious, always in danger of being superseded by reliance on coercive force and strength of numbers. Politics is achieved where enemies manage their conflict by talking, conciliation or negotiation. Politics in the proper sense requires that parties in conflict move away from the kind of emotional attitude towards enemies which can be characterized by contempt, hatred, desire for revenge, and preparedness to do harm. This is not an easy achievement, since no one doubts that these are understandable reactions towards enemies. The weak do what they have to do in order to survive; but that the stronger are prepared to make concessions, voluntarily to relinquish power when required, and otherwise to allow themselves to be bound by constitutional constraints is not to be taken for granted. The role of religious symbols such as the cross is crucial for evoking and motivating this distinctively human and political attitude.

What is politics?

Politics is one way of managing social conflict.[3] It is by no means the only way, and it may not even appear to be the most effective way of dealing with conflict. Conflict arises because the goals pursued by different people are mutually frustrating or incompatible. Conflict is socially significant when the number of people involved is large, typically when the goals pursued by different groups or classes or parties are mutually incompatible. Conflict can be managed by one group or party succeeding in imposing its will on the other group(s). This can occur through the actual use of or the threat of violence. However, experience shows that this is not an enduring or stable way to manage conflict (Schellenberg, 1982).

The management of conflict is political when it renounces such primary reliance on coercion and attempts to achieve conciliation through negotiation, argument and persuasion. Most typically, political management of conflict occurs within a territory which enjoys a form of rule, namely, a state. The key to politics, however, is not primarily the state institutions, but the reliance on talking and persuasion to achieve some accommodation between conflicted parties. The common use of the English word 'politics' is of the way in which interest groups compete for power within a state so as to pursue their interests as effectively as possible. Accordingly, the conflict element is carried over in the colloquial usage, but the reliance on non-violent means for managing conflict is not incorporated in the usual definition. For the purposes of analysis and argument, it is important to have some way of distinguishing between the handling of conflict which relies on talking or negotiation, and the handling of conflict which relies on force. I attempt to maintain this distinction by stressing that only some forms of state rule are political. There are many forms of rule which (a) deny the reality and inevitability of conflict and/or (b) attempt to eliminate or resolve conflict by force. Of course, the importance of the distinction does not entail that there can be a complete separation of these elements. Max Weber rightly emphasizes that a state must claim a monopoly on justified use of coercive force within its territory (Weber, 1919). Even a state which succeeded in handling conflict by negotiation would have to claim monopoly of legitimate use of force. And this claim would on occasion be invoked in practice when individuals or groups within the state attempted to achieve their interests by force at the expense of others or of the common good. Weber's definition picks out an unavoidable feature of a state, but does not claim to be exhaustive in its explanation of the state.

The political management of conflict will usually involve compromise. Not every party to a conflict can achieve the realisation of all its goals – otherwise there would not have been a conflict in the first place. This is one reason to speak of managing instead of resolving conflict. Conflict persists, but the achievement of politics is that the conflict is conducted by talking rather than with the use of force. Only where there is a willingness on all sides to forego some of their objectives can political accommodation be reached. It is not surprising if weaker parties are prepared to compromise: the willingness of an economically and militarily stronger party to enter into a compromise for the sake of a peaceful settlement is not to be presupposed. Of course the practice of politics requires considerable skill and a culture committed to managing its conflicts by political means will devote resources to cultivating those skills.

Conflict is understood in terms of incompatible goals. Goals are to be distinguished from ideals and values. A goal is a state of affairs which one hopes to bring about (e.g. free health care at the point of delivery). The state of affairs is capable of being described in all relevant features. By contrast, ideals or values such as justice, or peace, or compassion, can be invoked to make sense of one's motivation for wanting to bring about the quality of health care envisaged. Of themselves, the ideals or values are not capable of such precise description as is the case with goals.

Notoriously, people on opposite sides of a conflict can claim justice or peace or similar values to make sense of their position. Litigants who resort to courts hope to get justice, but until the court has decided the issue, parties in dispute presume that justice in the case lies with them. The point here is not to affirm that courts always succeed in doing justice; there are too many examples of blatant miscarriages of justice to make that case. Rather, the point is that many who invoke justice are not in agreement on what arrangements they judge as just: the appeal to justice does not provide common ground. Conflict is not resolved simply by parties in dispute espousing values and ideals such as justice. The language of values and ideals is aspirational, and it is not necessarily helpful for managing conflict. In fact, it can hinder the political dealing with conflict because an apparent agreement at the level of ideals may obscure the real differences of interests in what is proposed. For example, those who advocate the nationalization of the banks are opposed by free market proponents, but both sides make their case in terms of what is conducive to the good of the economy and the common good. Reference to the values of the public welfare or the common good does not decide the issue in favour of one or other goal.

The distinction between means and goals is also relevant, and it allows a further distinction between the technical and the practical. The practical has to do with goals, while the technical concentrates on means. Many of those who hold power in public office often prefer to see politics as a technical matter. Candidates present themselves to electorates as technicians, with the necessary competence to implement the measures which are means to the assumed goals (Crick 1982, Ch.5). The goals are assumed to be agreed, and are typically presented in non-controversial language: full employment, social welfare, education, health care, security. However, the assumption of agreement glosses over the real conflicts between incompatible goals, so the language of ideals and values short-circuits the process. Since all are assumed to want justice, peace, and prosperity, it appears that the only issue remaining is to decide on the means to be adopted to bring them about. And that issue reverts to the question of which professionals are most skilled and best placed to deliver the desired goals.

Some of those who theorise about politics reinforce this view that it is ultimately not a practical matter, about divergent goals, but a technical matter, about implementing the right means. Plato's vision of the philosopher king is one example, giving priority to the mastery of the knowledge whereby the city could be guided to good order, without allowing for the possibility that there might be validly diverging views about what would constitute good order. Machiavelli in *The Prince* also concentrated on the question of means, assuming the goals of the prince were given. Curiously, nationalists, republicans and socialists also tend to deny the practical nature of politics, because while they provide an analysis to explain the occurrence of conflict (incompatible goals), they aspire to a situation in which no conflict would occur. Marxists aim for a conflict free because classless society. Rousseauian republicans wish to suppress the kind of politics based on competing sectional interests and party factions to ensure a harmonious pursuit of the common good as found in the general will. Nationalists are confident that the people or nation, once allowed to rule itself, will be so unified that it will pursue its destiny without diverting from its chosen path. Anyone who might challenge this required unity is regarded thereby as disqualifying herself as a member of the nation, or people, or classless progressive society.

Knowledge

The poverty of the language available to our societies for managing conflict reflects general disregard for fundamental issues about the goods to be achieved in human society. These are the issues about what we want, how we want to live, what quality of relationships we desire to have with each other.[4] Our culture gives pre-eminence to the technical in many ways, but especially in our investment in knowledge. For the sake of what we might wish to do, to build and create, we invest a lot of effort in accumulating technical knowledge. This is primarily knowledge about materials, which enables us to exploit fossil fuels, wind and sun power, radioactive elements, optic fibre, microchip processors, and so on. The extent of our culture's investment in the accumulation of such knowledge is evident. There is no comparable investment by our culture in accumulating practical knowledge.

To know what people want and to know what conflicted parties want would require a mastery of the languages in which people express their convictions and values. These include the languages of religious world-views, in which people express their fundamental desires and their ultimate aspirations. A culture committed to managing conflict by political means would endeavour to be literate in what people want, what groups want, and in their relevant histories. This requires complex hermeneutic skills, since we should expect it to be the case that people want many things, that their goals are diverse and often conflicted. Accordingly, it is not a matter of having an established agreed principle or set of principles specifying a highest good or most fundamental set of needs from which guidance and directives might be drawn: that would be the model of technical knowledge.

Religious world-views and religious languages

Good people wanting to do good things are in conflict with one another, because the goals they pursue are incompatible. For instance, cabinet ministers seeking more resources for their departments are in conflict. More money for education means less for security, or social welfare, or health. Conflict occurs because of the richness of the human good, the creativity of human agents, and the limitations of time, energy and material resources for them to realise their plans and objectives. Of course, conflict also occurs because of greed, hatred, and the desire to dominate others. It is important that religious people and Christians in particular, be free of the prejudice that conflict arises only from fault or sin on the part of some participant in the conflict. This in itself can be a contribution to dialogue, to challenge the assumptions of the presence of guilt for wrongdoing. It is an important corrective for religious world-views to accept that conflict can also arise from good people wanting to do good things.

Just as there have been philosophical positions (e.g. Plato, Rousseau, Marx) which have discounted conflict, so too there are theological accounts often drawing on eschatological visions of God's Kingdom which regard conflict only in negative terms. Most religious visions with their associated ideals favour harmony, community, peace, between the Creator and creatures, between all humankind, all peoples and states, and between humans and the rest of creation. Christian rhetoric often appeals to values, ideals, and visions of the good, easily evoked by powerful symbols (swords into ploughshares, the heavenly banquet, the feeding of the multitude, the healing of the blind and lame). But the relevant values and ideals cannot function as premises in arguments from which governments or other authorities can deduce suitable policy proposals. Christians must take care that their invoking of their ideals not distract from or frustrate the work of building viable proposals based on reliable practical knowledge of the issues.

The danger in this case is that religious language plays down at least or even denies the reality of actual conflict, stressing instead the aspiration to harmony and community which it holds out as a promise. But the opposite danger is also linked to the use of religious language, namely, that it exacerbates conflict and polarizes the parties.

Religiously inspired languages can be problematic in the face of conflict. Instead of recognizing what is common to the conflicted parties the language of faith can stress instead the divisions, the differences between the insiders and the others. The familiar pairs of Jew and Gentile, believer and infidel, Christian and non-Christian, the *ummah* and the unbeliever convey the separation. Common to these examples is the use of terminology which originates within one world-view, and which is used by sharers in that world-view to speak of those who are outside.

If citizens of liberal polities wish to be political in the proper sense they require an appropriate language for conflict, in which parties in conflict can speak *to* each other, and not simply speak *about* each other. The dangers with the latter are many. One is that the speaker can be misled into depicting the opponent in terms which that opponent could not recognize. These terms can be loaded with presuppositions from one side of the polarization. Another is that the opponent can be treated as an object, to be described, evaluated, analysed and discussed, but not directly addressed. To speak *to*, and not simply *about*, each other in a conflict situation requires a degree of communality at least at the level of language. A shared language is required in which each in turn can have the status both of speaker and spoken to. It has to be a language that is rooted in a common humanity.

Is there a common language in each of these cases in which we can speak across the division, and not only about those on the other side? Secularists have long advocated their stance as providing the needed neutral ground, but the neutrality of that ground is suspect. MacIntyre among others has highlighted the illusion and the danger that people of faith may have sold the pass in conversations simply by accepting the ideology of a neutral language (1990). The politics of recognition and identity politics are built on the argument that the standard assumptions about the autonomous agent and the nature of practical rationality are not only not neutral as they claim, but that they privilege one kind of identity and mode of experience, that of the masculine, western individual (Taylor 1997, pp.225-256). However, the neutral language of the secularist is not the only stance. It is conceivable that the languages of faith themselves might still embrace a perspective which can recognize a common humanity beyond the divisions of faith allegiance. This more than anything else is the precondition for a political handling of fundamental conflict. Is it possible for people of religious conviction to transcend the divisiveness and polarization implicit and often explicit in their inherited languages without abandoning their religious worldview? Can Jews, Christians, Muslims, Hindus, Buddhists, etc., interact with each other as participants in conflict, committed to handling the conflict in a political manner? Is there a possible perspective, rooted in a shared humanity, which acknowledges the religious dimension of human experience, and so does not entail abandonment of deeply held convictions, but enables a speaking to opponents and not merely about them? To ask these questions is not to fall into the trap of accepting that religious difference is the principal source of conflict. William Cavanaugh identifies this danger that the modern liberal critique of religion as the source of conflict be accepted and confronts it directly. We do not have to adopt the thesis that conflict emanates primarily from religious differences in order to accept the propensity of faith movements to be divisive and to acknowledge the history of religious conflict, often violent in its expression (Cavanaugh 2005, pp.301-32).

Considering the elements in religious world-views which provide a foundation for dialogue across divisions it is possible to identify clearly a number of instances which have facilitated the articulation of a genuinely human value or concern. One of these, the Decalogue, was recognized already in medieval conversations as expressing the moral preconditions for human society. Recent literature has returned to this insight. I review this example, but suggest in turn that the Cross can be considered in the same manner, as evoking a human reality which anyone can find helpful, whether Christian or not. This is not an argument about historical influences, or causation. It is not raising claims to ownership of ideas or priorities in recognition. It is simply looking at the content of some elements of religious world-views and finding there dimensions of human truth and value.[5]

The human wisdom of the Decalogue

'Keeping human life human' is a slogan coined by Reformed Christian theologian, Paul L. Lehmann. Lehmann had four books published, the last one posthumously (1940, 1963, 1975, 1995). They all reflect his interest in the practical demands of Christianity, and a concern with the political implications of Christian faith. He had been a friend of Dietrich Bonhoeffer, and his own political involvement included resistance to the MacCarthyism of 1950s America and engagement in the campaign for civil rights. Nancy J. Duff worked with Lehmann on the Decalogue book and edited it for publication after his death. She explains that the subtitle of the book carried a longstanding theme of Lehmann's writing and teaching: 'making and keeping human life human'.

The commandments delivered by Moses are seen as humanizing forces in the face of dehumanizing pressures on human life. Relationships of domination in which power oppresses threaten to dehumanize both oppressors and victims. Duff explains that the commandments 'have to do with how power is wielded among human beings – whether that means labourers who need time to rest, elderly parents who need to be honoured, or the poor who have been falsely accused and need to be defended in court.' (2009, pp.41-2) With this emphasis on how power is exercised, the commandments' demands are addressed to the powerful. They protect the interests of the weak and vulnerable, but in such a way that the onus is on the powerful to secure their interests rather than on the weaker party to fight for their entitlements.

This twentieth century approach to the Decalogue has its precedents in the medieval thesis that what Moses enjoined on the people as divine law was identical to what human reason might know as requirements of natural law. Thomas Aquinas was not alone among medieval authors in spelling out the relationship between what human reason knows by its own lights and what it is instructed to do by revelation of Divine will or by human made law. From a very general precept that 'no one should harm another', derived from the basic orientation of practical reason that 'good is to be done and pursued and evil avoided', Aquinas recognized that the injunctions of the second tablet of the Decalogue made this more precise, not to kill, not to steal, not to falsely accuse, not to violate the marital commitments of the other (Porter, 2009). Although presented in the biblical literature as part of God's covenant with his chosen people, and so part of divinely revealed law, Aquinas considered that its general precepts were consistent with what humans were capable of knowing apart from special revelation, relying on the revelation of the good implicit in creation itself. In other words, violation of those norms prohibiting killing, theft, perjury and adultery could be seen as a practical denial of a common humanity. Such a violation would be tantamount to the assertion that the other, the stranger or the enemy, is not entitled to that respect or recognition which anyone demands for oneself.

Alasdair MacIntyre has elaborated on this thought in the context of contemporary disputes about what is owed to others. The context for his reflection is the failure to find agreement on the fundamental principles regulating social existence, also because the ethical theories espoused by different people are so incompatible. This experience provokes the question whether there is in fact a natural law rooted in a common human nature. MacIntyre answers this challenge by reflecting on the preconditions for rational engagement between adherents of competing and opposed world-views (2009). Wanting to avoid a situation in which power determines outcomes, the only option for reasonable people is to enter into dialogue despite their differences which are so fundamental as to make all dialogue problematic. Such discourse will not be possible unless participants are bound by rules. MacIntyre argues that 'we will only be able to enquire together with such others in a way that accords with the canons of rationality, if both we and they treat as binding upon us a set of rules that turn out to be just those enjoined by the natural law.' (p.3)

This argument echoes the introduction of the concept of virtue in MacIntyre's earlier work, *After Virtue* (1984) in which he argued that the cardinal virtues of justice, temperance, fortitude and prudence were just those acquired qualities which were needed if participants in practices were to realise the internal goods of those practices. Now it turns out that 'the set of precepts conformity to which is a precondition for shared rational enquiry as to how our practical disagreements are to be resolved have the same content as those precepts that Aquinas identified as the precepts of the natural law' (MacIntyre 2009, p.23). The precepts in question are Aquinas's fundamental practical principle that the good is to be done and pursued, that the relevant human goods are the goods of survival, of life, and of knowledge and social order. The shared enquiry required for the reasonable resolution of intractable moral disagreements would have to recognize the good of truth as constitutive of the human good. The pursuit of truth, MacIntyre suggests, could not simply be instrumentalized to other goods, and would have to be given a place in the overall plan of human life and activity, supported by appropriate virtues and rules (pp.20-4). The pursuit of truth is jeopardized by the attraction of power, money and pleasure, which can undermine the clarity of focus on the good, and this attraction should be checked by the cultivation of an intellectual and moral asceticism.

Acknowledging that the pursuit of truth in the context of disagreement is precarious, the open and self-critical engagement with others must presuppose a trust that one will not be attacked, robbed, lied to, or otherwise taken advantage of. These expectations, when articulated as precepts, are identified as preconditions for rational enquiry, and so are not known as a result of enquiry. Here MacIntyre sees further the parallel to Aquinas's claims for the precepts of the natural law. His conditions for rational enquiry are like Aquinas's precepts, universal in scope, exceptionless, and the same for everyone. He concludes that theoretical argument cannot provide justification for these precepts, but can attempt to show that they are presupposed by rational enquiry, and that any practical enquiry 'which does not presuppose them fails in rationality' (p.24).

MacIntyre is not naïve about the possibilities of rational discourse, since he stresses the threats which arise from the distorting pull of power, wealth and pleasure. Accordingly the asceticism and self-discipline of participants in managing the 'partialities and prejudices' arising from 'material and psychological interests' are among the preconditions of shared rational enquiry (p.22).

Apart from the attractions of power, wealth and pleasure, the psychological pressures will include hatred of enemies, desire for revenge, intention to oppress and do down opponents. How might opponents who come with such baggage begin the process of politics with one another, entering into rational discourse and abiding by the norms which MacIntyre articulates? Does his proposed asceticism suffice, even for those who acknowledge its cogency? A reconstruction of the human meaning of the cross by analogy with the human interpretation of the Ten Commandments offers a partial answer to this question.

The cross points the way
The New Testament scholar N. T. Wright maintains that the modern separation of religion and politics is foreign to the situation in which Jesus lived and acted. A religious movement such as that led by Jesus of Nazareth was at the same time a political phenomenon. Wright argues further that the death of Jesus cannot be completely understood unless it is situated in its political context. He approaches the events surrounding Jesus' life and death using the methods and techniques of the historian (Wright, 1996). The New Testament records and other literature are treated in exactly the same way that other historical data would be treated. In particular the history of Josephus provides a useful touchstone for the use of such texts. Josephus reports on political movements and their leaders during Second Temple Judaism and this provides the historian with a context for situating Jesus and his movement. Wright interprets the story of Jesus against the background of a series of leaders who sought to lead a revolt against the Roman domination of the Holy Land. He stresses that the religious meaning of such would-be Messiahs cannot be separated from their political significance. In other

words, Jesus is to be understood not merely but also as a religious-political leader, who started a movement like others, but unlike them in at least one important respect. The significant difference is in the way in which Jesus died. All other messianic leaders failed in their efforts at revolt and were executed, but they failed having attempted an armed resistance to the occupying power. As Wright put it, Jesus was executed by the Romans because he was a political rebel who posed a threat to Roman dominance, but he was handed over for execution by his own people because he was not a political rebel as they would have wanted him to be. Wright stresses the difference in Jesus' refusal to attempt a reinstatement of the Kingdom of God in Israel using the means and instruments of force.

Without explicitly drawing the distinction between two meanings of political, as I have done above, Wright is nonetheless operating with the same distinction. We see how in his discussion the two meanings of political are invoked, as also the tension between them. With the usual meaning of the term, political refers to the competition for power, and the mastery of control in the rule or government of a state. This includes also the use of military means to capture and maintain power. Other leaders during Second Temple Judaism were political in this sense; Jesus was not. His movement was political in the more precise sense of rejecting reliance on armed force to attain desired goals. And his goals were political in a theological sense having to do with the Reign of God, deliverance from Exile, and the restoration of Temple worship.

Wright lays considerable emphasis on the theme of 'return from exile' maintaining that the restoration of temple worship following the ending of the Babylonian captivity had not fulfilled the promise. As long as the people with a sense of election knew themselves to be subject to foreign and domestic powers they had the sense that they were still in exile, still waiting to be restored to the situation in which God ruled. Hence, the sense of messianic expectancy, when this promised deliverance would occur. Several possible messiahs attempted to fulfil the role relying on armed rebellion. Jesus is to be seen in this context of messianic expectancy, and his words and deeds are intelligible as proclamation that the promised deliverance had arrived. In contrast to other leaders who seemed to offer hope of a deliverance from foreign oppression, a restoration of covenantal order in which the people could serve its God in a coherent manner, Jesus stood out for his clarity about the futility of opposing foreign domination as a means to realising the kingdom of God. The judgment of God communicated by Jesus was not directed against the foreign power, but against God's own people for failing to be the 'light of the nations'. The Roman hegemony was the most recent in a series, as Wright underlines – 'the stories that formerly featured Egypt, Babylon, and Syria now focused on Rome' – but the path to deliverance proclaimed by Jesus did not require a defeat of the occupying power.

> "He [Jesus] and his contemporaries were living within a controlling story, a great scriptural narrative through which the puzzles of their own times could be discerned (though how this should be done, and what might be the results of doing so, were of course fiercely contested). The controlling story was often told in terms of the new Exodus: when the Egypts of the day, not least their Pharaohs, vaunted themselves against God's people, God would deliver Israel by mighty acts within history, and bring his people through their great trials to vindication at last." (Wright 2000, pp.29-30)

Jesus' announcement of the Kingdom of God, and the claim to heal and forgive sin are the two sides of the same coin: forgiveness and healing mark the end of the exile of the people from God, and the kingdom marks the beginning of the new reign in which all is rightly ordered according to God's will. So much for the similarities. What marks Jesus out in contrast to the other revolutionaries is his explicit refusal to resort to military force or violence in order to initiate the kingdom. He accepts his victimhood as the consequence of refusal to meet force with force, and at the same time his execution shows to all who would hope to follow a nationalistic project of restoration what fate would await them. Like other leaders of reform and restoration movements Jesus was killed. But unlike other such leaders he died proclaiming forgiveness for his enemies. He accepted the violence done to him, but refused to respond in kind, he refused to use violence to achieve his aims.

The human meaning of the cross

To recognize the significance of the cross in the context of the non-violent managing of conflict does not require any profession of Christian faith. That recognition merely presupposes an appreciation of the human achievement which is politics, as institutionalized in many forms of constitutional, liberal democracy. To be political is to accept the prevalence of conflict, to perceive the threat to one's own interests yet renounce a reliance on coercive force to secure them, and to commit to managing the conflict in institutions sustaining negotiation and conciliation. Whoever is political in this sense is capable of recognizing the human significance of Jesus' cross. Of course Jesus of Nazareth was neither the first nor the last to be crucified. It was a standard form of execution in the Roman world. But it is appropriately associated with Jesus because of the way in which he accepted execution. He was not executed because he was a defeated rebel. His being polite, his embrace of politics in the proper sense led to the consequence of his being victimized. The abandonment of a desire for revenge, for retaliation, the willingness to move ahead with former enemies, even to offer them friendship, the renunciation of an armed campaign, these are the marks of a political attitude in the fuller, more human sense of politics.

The political handling of conflict is a wonderful human achievement. Parliaments, courts and the institutions of industrial relations exemplify how participants in conflict have learned to manage their conflict by talking. However, to date it has not been a universal achievement, and where it has emerged it is a precarious achievement. There is always the inclination to resort to superior numbers and greater force in order to achieve one's interests. There is always the temptation to regard the weaknesses of opponents as grounds for assuming that force will be effective. There is always the impatience felt by the men and women of action with talk-shops which seem to get nowhere.

In the face of such powerful emotions and motivations, the doing of politics in the proper sense requires an equally powerful motivation which enables people to overcome their bitterness, hatred and spontaneous aggression and begin to talk to their opponents. This is the context in which the example of the one who did not respond in kind to his persecutors is relevant. If humans are to be political, and manage their conflicts by talking, instead of by force and coercion, they need a similar attitude towards their enemies. The required attitude must be strong enough to overcome spontaneous emotional responses; it would require a real dying to oneself. The cross is a reminder of what it costs to be political, it is a reminder that politics is possible, and it invites a commitment to handle conflict by talking.

Conclusion

There are three important concepts in the topic of this paper: cross, politics, and language. In each case an important distinction is drawn between two senses in which the concept is used. I distinguish between different but related languages. There is language available for communicating within a shared world-view, and there is language available for speaking across the divides between world-views. What is spoken across the divide must be rooted in the world-view and be faithful to it. In other words, there is a language we use for speaking to co-religionists *about* others, and there is a language we use for speaking *to* others, who do not share our world-view. Politics is also distinguished, following Aristotle, who uses the same term to name the full field of activity, and the very best form of that activity (1972). Politics names the study of all the constitutional forms, and it names the optimal constitution. The defective or deficient constitutions diverge from the best as the standard against which they are compared and with which they are measured. The contemporary application of this is to locate the best instance in those forms of rule which manage conflict by talking, and the deficient forms rely on force and violence to deal with conflict. The cross of Jesus is spoken of in two senses also. There is the full theological meaning of the death of Christ, about which theologians and believers can have differing views, and there is the human significance of the event, knowledge of which does not presuppose faith.

My argument is that politics in the precise sense demands the kind of commitment made by Jesus which led to his execution, and so the discourse of the cross conveys a message about the human preconditions of politics.

Politics, based on a commitment to manage and handle conflict by talking, is an admirable human achievement. It is also precarious, since there are many pressures, especially on those who are stronger, either in military terms or in terms of numbers, to rely on their greater power to achieve their interests. Resistance to those pressures requires not only a valuing of the human achievement of politics, but also a self-discipline in mastery of emotional responses and immediacy of interests. Assuming such transcendence of personal preference, parties in conflict will furthermore require a language reflecting the horizon of a shared humanity and overcoming the divisiveness which inheres in some traditional and religious world-views. They will have to be able to talk *to* and not merely *about* each other. Nevertheless they will require sufficient talk about the other so that a grasp of the needs, goals, wants and ambitions of the other can feed into a serious engagement about the incompatible goals which constitute their conflict. The reality of that conflict should not jeopardize the sense of moral obligation to recognize and respect the humanity of the enemy. Who can enter into dialogue without minimal assurance that they will not be killed, defrauded, violated or deceived? The precepts of the second tablet of the Decalogue articulate the preconditions to which enemies must conform if they are to engage in a political management of their conflict. However, there are more strenuous demands made by politics in the full sense. These demands can hardly be met unless parties in conflict are sufficiently distanced from their own interests and preferences that they can allow these to be subjected to rigorous assessment and demand for justification. Such transcending of one's subjectivity is tantamount to a loss of self.

The demand that the cross be removed from public places is only meaningful in contexts which have learned to manage conflict by talking, in parliaments, in courts, under the rule of law. Only where the human message of the cross has been learned and institutionalized in practices (not necessarily learned *from* the cross) can one seek protection of one's own world-view and equality of respect from public authorities. Considering this irony, it seems that the places of conflict such as Israel and Palestine need the reminder of this human reality, that the human achievement of a political and non-military handling of the conflict will require the adoption of such an attitude to enemies as was shown by the political leader Jesus of Nazareth. There is no avoiding this challenge. The invitation to take up their cross is the human challenge to all parties in conflict. Keeping human life human requires not only adherence to the basic moral precepts which can enable enemies to enter into negotiation with one another; this is respect for the human dignity and basic rights of the other. Keeping human life human will require also an abandonment of the willingness to resort to violence, a preparedness to compromise and a renunciation of self-preference.

---

[1] I acknowledge that Christians differ with regard to the crucifix. In this paper I write of both, since the one element of the complex human meaning of the death of Christ on which I focus is evoked by both cross and crucifix. However, I do not restrict my remarks to the cross, as a shared symbol among all Christians, since the figure of Jesus suffering on the cross is also relevant to the point.

[2] In November 2009 the European Court of Human Rights issued a judgment that crucifixes in classrooms in Italian state schools constituted a violation of religious and educational freedoms. The Court affirmed that state schools had to observe confessional neutrality, and refrain from imposing beliefs. With this judgment the European Court overturned the decision of the Italian courts which had rejected the claim of a Finnish resident in Northern Italy that her children were discriminated against by the public display of the crucifix.

[3] In this I follow Crick (1982), who offers a revision of Aristotle's approach to politics.

[4] The referents of 'we' in this and similar sentences are the citizens of political systems.

[5] An eminent example of this approach is the study by Roger Ruston (2004) linking the concept of human rights from political discourse with the biblical notion of the image of God.

I Am – for You

Clare Amos

I was privileged to be part of the international team that wrote the Bible Studies for the 2008 Lambeth Conference. We had been asked by the Archbishop of Canterbury to take the Gospel of John as the biblical book to explore, but within that parameter we were invited to choose the 'theme' we wanted to focus on and invited to make our own selection of texts for the bishops to study. After some discussion we chose to look at the 'I am' passages in John's Gospel – but with a bit of a twist. Most people are aware of the seven obvious 'I am' passages in the Gospel, where Jesus compares himself with common physical realities such as 'Light' or 'Bread', 'Life' or 'Vine'. Considerably fewer are aware of the other 'I am' passages of this Gospel, which appear without an apparent predicate, and where even the words 'I am' are sometimes half hidden by the English translation (although the NRSV translation often draws our attention to the words via footnotes). Since we had to offer a total of 15 Bible studies for the bishops over the course of the two-and-a-half-week Lambeth conference, it was fortunate that we had these additional 'I am' passages to incorporate. Additionally, as theological educators, since part of our aim was to challenge the bishops to discover for themselves new insights into scripture, we felt that it was valuable to be able to draw to their attention these extra occurrences of 'I am'. One of these extra 'I am' sayings, although in this particular instance it is hardly half-hidden because it shrieks at us from the page with a startling clash of Greek tenses, comes at the end of John 8: 'Jesus said to them, "Very truly I tell you, before Abraham was, I am".' (8.58)

This passage, which has been called 'the towering crest of Jesus' claim for himself (Price 1996, pp.148, 158), comes at the end of a long chapter in which several 'hidden' examples of 'I am' have previously appeared, and is clearly intended as a significant point of climax in the Gospel. It was therefore important that we included it in our 'I am' collection for the Bible Studies. In many ways however it would have been easier to omit this passage. Why is this? Because this assertion comes at the end of a passage in which the discussion between Jesus and a group described as 'the Jews' has become increasingly fractious. Both Jesus and his opponents are given horribly hostile words to speak: in 8.48 'the Jews' charge Jesus, 'Are we not right in saying that you are a Samaritan and have a demon', but that has come after Jesus' own words to the group of Jews, 'You are from your father the devil'(8.44). The acrimonious exchange, and particularly the words placed upon Jesus' lips, is an embarrassment to many modern Christians, even those such as myself who believe that in this dialogue we are listening to the debates from Church and synagogue at the end of the 1st century AD rather than the *ipsissima verba* of Jesus Christ in his human life. For even if this is the case, phrases such as the description of Jewish people as the 'devil's children' have played a significant role in the tortured relationship between Christianity and Judaism over the last 200 years. The phrase has been frequently employed by Christians when they have wanted to attack Jews and Judaism. There was a picture-book for children published by the Nazis in Germany in 1936 which included a cartoon of a Jewish person and the caption 'The father of the Jews is the devil.' Four centuries earlier Martin Luther had spoken of the Jews as being 'the devil's people'. In other words Christian interpretations of texts like 8.43-50 bear at least some responsibility for the long history of anti-Semitism which culminated in the Nazi Holocaust.

Some scholars argue that though such texts as 8.43-50 may

have been used by Christians as a weapon in their hatred of Jews – that is to misunderstand and misuse them. But in reality it is not that simple, and such an argument can feel very like special pleading. There is a damning comment by a Jewish scholar which has to be taken seriously when we read passages like this in John's Gospel, 'Without Christianity's New Testament, Hitler's Mein Kampf could never have been written.' (Berkovitz 1978, p.325) The Christian writer Roy Eckhardt calls John 8.44-47 'the road to Auschwitz' (quoted in Freudman 1994, p.267).

So to explore 8.58 within the wider context of John 8 – particularly in a high profile context such as the Lambeth Conference – felt like a risky undertaking. Inevitably Anglican relationships with other churches and other faiths would form part of the Conference agenda, and it would not be helpful if our exploration of such a difficult text encouraged in any way a naïve anti-Judaism. Being someone who is both committed to working towards a mature and considered relationship between Christianity and Judaism, and someone who is by nature also something of a masochist, I offered, when we divided up passages for work in our Bible study team, to work on this text. It was, however, also salutary for me to discover that my sensitivities about the text were not entirely shared by all other members of our international team: concern about anti-Judaism in the New Testament is very much a western preoccupation, due of course in part to our particular history of Jewish-Christian relations.

One of the questions I needed to explore as I began to work on the passage (we decided to take John 8.31-59 as its parameters), was 'What is the connection between these two: the high point of that spectacular claim of Jesus in 8.58, and that low point of the vicious debate a few verses earlier?' And what does that mean for us as we read this chapter today?

Early on in my work I came across the comment of Rosemary Radford Ruether that anti-Judaism in the New Testament is 'the left hand of Christology' (Ruether 1974, p.246). The harsh words of John 8.44-47 can be viewed as the other side of the coin to the assertion of Jesus' identity with God that seems to be proclaimed in 8.58. The high point and the low point belong together. Ruether suggests that this means that we might need to be willing to alter how we express our belief in Jesus Christ.

But can we not explore whether John's 'high Christology' can in fact assist us to a deeper understanding of this problematic text – and through it to ways of engaging with Scripture? And if so, this means that it is an important question to explore not only for those (such as Europeans and North Americans) for whom engaging with Judaism as a living faith is a part of past history and present context, but also for all Christians through the world – even in regions where few Jewish people live today. All of us need to recall that interpreting the Bible is a potentially dangerous pursuit – which can on occasion sadly and ironically become death-dealing rather than life-giving.

At this point I need to digress to explore exactly what may be being implied by the 'I am' statements in John's Gospel, both at 8.58 and more widely. There is wide-spread agreement that such first person claims are a deliberate echo by Jesus of the key passage in Exodus 3.1-15 where the name of God is disclosed to Moses. The name that is apparently disclosed is YHWH, often vocalised, especially in Christian scholarship, as Yahweh. However alongside the revelation of the actual name in Exodus 3.15, the name is explained by the phrase 'I am who I am' in the previous verse, and this is then reinforced by the command given to Moses to tell the Israelites that 'I am has sent me to you,' which parallels what will be commanded in verse 15, but simply using the phrase 'I am' rather than the word YHWH. So a close link seems to be being made between 'I am' and God's name YHWH, two words which in any case in Hebrew share several letters in common. But what is the actual meaning or etymology of the name YHWH? Although not absolutely proven, it is highly likely that the word YHWH does in fact have a genuine etymological link to a form of the verb 'to be', so that what is expressed in the first person as 'I am' in Exodus 3.14 is then reinforced by being repeated in a 3rd person form as YHWH.

The meaning of names mattered, certainly in the biblical period – they told you something important about the person being described. So Jacob was a 'heel' or trickster because his name *Ya'aqov* included within it the Hebrew word for 'heel' *'aqov* and Isaac or *Yitzhaq* was so called because 'laughter', *tzahaq* was associated with his birth. So what does the name YHWH tell us about the God being so described? Both a great deal – and very little. For if God's name is linked in some way to the verb 'to be', 'being' is a notoriously fluid concept. Does it seek to emphasise God's eternal existence (which was the interpretation given by the translators of the Septuagint), does it speak of his active presence or of his power to sustain the world, or is it stressing God's role as creator (which attracts a number of scholars, who suggest that the word YHWH is a causative form of the verb 'to be' i.e. 'to make to be')?

Yet the very fluidity of the concept is itself making a key point about the Old Testament understanding of God – particularly in the light of the context in which the name is revealed in Exodus 3. Because names told you about the nature of someone – they also gave you a power over that person. If that was true for humans, how much more so for divine beings. To know the name of a God enabled you to 'call upon' him (or her) and to seek to bend them to your will. Such a view of the relationship between humanity and the divine is anathema to much of the spirituality of the Old Testament. There is therefore a great reticence about revealing God's name – for example when Jacob requested to know the name of his night-time divine assailant at the Fords of Penuel the request was ignored (Genesis 32.22-32). There is equally a determination that the name, once known, must not be abused. So the third of the 10 commandments specifically prohibits such misuse. God had needed to reveal his name to Moses in Exodus 3 – or else his people would have remained forever slaves in Egypt. However in choosing to reveal a name that is in some senses 'no name', or as the song-writer Brian Wren puts it 'an uncompleted name' (1973), God was insisting on preserving sovereign divine freedom – refusing to allow himself to be 'controlled' by those he was drawing to worship him. This is what the writer Eugene Peterson says about the revelation of the name.

> 'This God-revealing name, and the understandings that developed as it was used in prayer and obedience by the Hebrew people marks the deconstruction of every kind and sort of impersonal, magical, manipulative, abstract, coercive way of understanding God....A verb-dominated, life-emphatic sentence... God cannot be defined. 'Yahweh' is not a definition. God cannot be reduced to an object... Is the name purposely enigmatic – I think so. Revelational but not telling everything... disclosing intimacy, personal presence, but preserving mystery, forbidding possession and control?' (Peterson 2005, pp. 157, 159)

One of the quests of Old Testament scholarship in the middle of the twentieth century, particularly among German scholars, was the search for the theological centre of the Old Testament. A number of suggestions were offered – for example Walther Eichrodt argued that it was 'covenant', and Gerhard Von Rad linked it to 'salvation history'. Both these suggestions have considerable attraction – yet ultimately they fall short, for there are significant parts of the Old Testament, in particular the wisdom literature, that seem to fall outside the parameters of either 'covenant' or 'salvation history'. However another of the 'great

Germans', Walther Zimmerli, explored the question in a rather different way. Zimmerli argued that the centre and unifying focus of the Old Testament is to be discovered in the Old Testament understanding of the name of God as YHWH – and all that this implies In other words this gracious uncontrollability of God is itself a theme which runs through all strands of the Old Testament and draws them together, even in their differences, into the one canon (1978). Obviously Zimmerli gives attention to the actual revelation of the Name of God, and the laws such as the prohibitions against its misuse, which we looked at briefly above. However he also draws attention to other ways that human beings can try and 'capture' God, and how the God depicted in the Old Testament responds to these. For example there was the building of a temple in Jerusalem, which became all too easily a box in which God could be domesticated for the benefit of worshippers, and for the safety of the city of Jerusalem. In response to such attempts at control, God the 'I am who I am', according to exilic prophets such as Jeremiah and Ezekiel, chose to abandon city and temple and become a God without a home. The temple in Jerusalem was a physical box in which to confine God – but there were other perhaps more subtle containers in which humans could make their attempts at confinement. Perhaps the most important among these was the traditional 'moral equation' that inflexibly linked prosperity and failure to human behaviour. Yet once again prophetic voices such as Jeremiah break the box and make it clear that God will not be confined by any neat or limited human understandings of good and evil. As Zimmerli himself put it,

> 'The God who is invoked by the name "Yahweh" repeatedly demonstrates his freedom by dashing to pieces all the 'images' in which humanity would confine him. This takes place not only in Ex. 3:14, in the account of how the divine name is

revealed to Moses, but to an equal degree in the great prophets, or in the realm of wisdom, in Ecclesiastes and Job.' (Zimmerli 1978, p.14)

Of course the danger with such an 'apophatic' view of God is that, if taken to extremes, it can lead to the suggestion that we cannot know anything about God. If that is the case then God would be completely 'nameless' – which presumably would undermine the very purpose of his revelation of his name. Zimmerli guards against this interpretation by pointing out that the Old Testament suggests that there are two ways in particular that we can know something about the nature of God who is YHWH. The first is through history and the second is by his laws. In relation to the first Zimmerli points out the formula '… then they will know that I am YHWH', is generally preceded by the description of a historically measurable event. Such a formula occurs in a number of prophetic texts, and in parts of the Book of Exodus. In relation to law Zimmerli draws attention to parts of the Holiness Code in the Book of Leviticus, where a law is preceded or followed by the bald and apparently unlinked sentence. 'I am YHWH'. So history and law give us a vital clue to God's nature – but still allow God the freedom to be 'I am who I am'. However ultimately it seems to me that Zimmerli is suggesting that the God who identifies himself with the name YHWH or 'I am' consistently insists on his right to sit in judgement upon our cherished religious and moral traditions and perceptions.

It is this that I want to bear in mind as I now return to John's Gospel, first to 8.58, and then also to give attention to the 'hidden I am' of 4.26. Traditionally we have been so quick to draw the connection between these 'I am' sayings of Jesus and Jesus' claim to divinity that we have failed to notice the possible twist in the tale. For if God's revelation as YHWH 'I am' in the Old Testament offers a challenge to a comfortable and controlling understanding of who God is, if indeed as Eugene Peterson suggests 'it is purposely enigmatic ....[and] preserves mystery', (2005, p.159) then perhaps Jesus' assertion here in 8.58 needs also to be read in this light. And that we have singularly failed to do. And so if Jesus identifies himself as 'I am', is he not in the same breath calling into question all the absolute claims and certainties that traditional Christology has associated with him, and which Christians through the centuries have wanted to make on his behalf?

Within the framework of the narrative, Jesus as 'I am' is critiquing the sense of certainty displayed by those portrayed as his opponents. Earlier in the passage he had spoken of the 'truth that will set you free' (John 8.32), but certainty about one's tradition and the inability to hear the critique of others, is not that kind of freedom. Those with whom Jesus is apparently engaging were so sure of their own identity as Abraham's children that it had become a sort of possession – which both held them captive and excluded others, such as the Samaritans. Yet Christian readers of the story must never be tempted to stop there, and simply turn the passage into a form of apparently anti-Jewish rhetoric.

Because Jesus is also standing in judgment on Christian self-understanding. For Jesus to say of himself 'Before Abraham was, I am' is to assert a claim that relativises all the 'absolute' claims linked to religion that human beings might make, whether in the past, present or future. There is a plea here for us all to be more than we imagine ourselves to be, beyond the constraints of our tradition and identity. Can we say that his claim 'I am' critiques our own cherished religious traditions and institutions – perhaps even how we use the Bible, or how we think of the Church? Could this also mean that this claim of Jesus can answer (at least in part) the dilemma over those difficult verses (e.g. verses 44-47) namely that Jesus as 'I Am' actually requires us to reflect anew on how we use our Bible? Raymond Brown puts it like this: "Sooner or later Christian believers must wrestle with the limitations imposed on the Scriptures by the circumstances in which they were written." (1975, p.131)

To return therefore to the remarks of Rosemary Radford Ruether, even as we acknowledge that Christology can be the 'left hand' of anti-Judaism, perhaps we need to suggest that Christology can (or should) also become a valuable tool to challenge any anti-Judaic attitudes within the church.

Indeed it is interesting that in the other passages from John's Gospel which I want to explore – John 4.5-42, within the narrative Jesus actually comments that 'Salvation is from the Jews'. (John 4.22). And it is intriguing that there is another link between John 8 and John 4. For the critique directed at Jesus by his opponents includes the comment, 'Are we not right in saying that you are a Samaritan?' (John 8.48). Is this intended as a hint that we should somehow 'read' alongside each other these two episodes which are the only occasions in John's Gospel when the word 'Samaritan' is used? What can we discover if we do indeed make this connection? It is indeed intriguing to note that there is some evidence that interest in the nature and meaning of God's name was a particular feature of Samaritan faith (due in part to the focus on Moses that is so central to Samaritan history and tradition).[1]

Having contributed to the writing of the 2008 Lambeth Conference Bible studies, and participated in the Conference itself in a variety of ways, I became part of a minor industry that developed around the Anglican Communion over the next year or so – viz being invited into a variety of contexts to share my 'wisdom' about the event. Given my particular involvement it is not surprising that I normally focused on the Bible Studies.

I used to enjoy beginning my talk by asking the groups I was speaking to identify which is the first 'I am' saying in John's Gospel. People thought about it, and came up with a variety of answers. Some mentioned 'I am the Light of the World', others 'I am the Bread of Life'. I have to confess that it is with great glee that I chortled at these responses and told people that they were wrong. It is certainly true that 'I am the Bread of Life' in chapter 6 is the first 'I am with a predicate' in the Gospel, but in fact there are two earlier 'I am' sayings, which, although they are picked up in the marginal footnotes of many modern translations, are not immediately obvious to the English reader.

In fact the first 'I am' of John's Gospel occurs in John 4.26 – at a key moment in the dialogue between Jesus and the woman he meets at the well of Samaria. In the NRSV translation it is presented as 'I am he, the one speaking with you' – but actually in Greek it is simply 'I am the one speaking with you'.

'I am, the one speaking with you'. This is the first time that Jesus says 'I am' in the Gospel of John. I find it an exhilarating and powerful discovery to realise that the first time that Jesus discloses this divine identity it should be to a person who is a woman, a Samaritan, who was not a member of his own religious community, and someone who was apparently ostracised among her own people. What is this telling us about the nature of God? The disclosure comes at the end of a quite lengthy talk between Jesus and the woman, in which they have discussed theology almost as equals. In the course of their meeting, each has ministered to the other, new life has been offered, barriers have been broken and the vision of a new and deeper relationship between God and human beings, and between human beings themselves has been opened up. And then Jesus says 'I am'.

It is I think no accident that this first 'I Am' of John's Gospel is embedded in a passage which speaks so extensively about the barriers that existed between Jews and Samaritans. At the time of Jesus the primary quarrel between the two communities was focused on the two temples that were the focal buildings of each faith. As the woman said to Jesus, 'Our ancestors worshipped on this mountain – Gerizim – which rises high in the heart of

Samaritan territory – while you, the Jews, say that it is in the temple in Jerusalem that people need to worship God.'. So two holy places originally erected to venerate God had become focal points for hostility and division as both communities sought to possess God each on its own terms. They had become, if you like, the antithesis of allowing God the freedom to be God, to be YHWH the 'I am who I am'. It is into the middle of this bitter strife that Jesus reveals himself as 'I am', the very revelation of this name perhaps acting as judgement upon religious communities which sought to domesticate God, to claim that they and they alone had the whole truth, and who by their exclusion of others sought to limit God's freedom to act how, where and when he wishes. It is also no coincidence I think that the physical symbol that runs through the dialogue between Jesus and the woman is 'living water'. In Semitic languages, such as Hebrew, the normal expression for 'running water' – fresh water that comes from a spring rather than still, and possible contaminated, water from a well – is *mayim haim* which literally means 'living water'. The Gospel writer is deliberately punning on the dual possibilities of the expression. So when in verse 10 Jesus offers the woman 'living water', understandably her first thought is of such fresh gushing spring water. But the quality of such water – just as the quality of the 'I am' – is that it runs free; it is not under the control of human power. Like the Spirit of God 'living water' will run and blow where it –rather than we – wills.

And yet by God's grace human beings are a central part of this story. Jesus' first words to the woman are 'Give me a drink', expressing his thirst, his need, and asking this apparently unclean woman to meet it. For many Christians in Asia, especially in India, who come from disadvantaged groups and classes and are often treated as unclean in their societies, this encounter expresses the very heart of the Christian Gospel. Significantly it is one of the most depicted gospel stories in Asian Christian art. To be willing to receive water from another in such a culture is to show respect to the giver – to break down the barriers between the clean and unclean. So Jesus' engagement with the woman breaks the societal protocols of division and leads to a mutual liberation both for the woman and for himself; his thirst for righteousness is quenched by his valuing of the woman.

Jean Vanier puts it like this: 'I am' begs for water from one of the most despised and broken women, who is no one, with no name, who is nothing in the eyes of society. Jesus reveals to her who she is and who she will become – a source of the waters of life of God – if she opens up her heart to him and receives his love. Misery and mercy meet in love.' (Vanier 2004, p.98)

I do not think there is a better visual expression of this truth than the statue called the 'Water of Life' which is found in the grounds of Chester Cathedral. It offers a profound depiction of the sense of mutuality and interdependence at the heart of the story. Who is ministering to whom? Surely we cannot separate out the giving and receiving – both are dependent each on the other. What a gospel we are being offered!

One of the reasons I enjoy talking to groups of people about the Bible is that often I discover fresh insights from those I am meeting with. As part of my post-Lambeth Conference 'tour' I had been invited to speak to a group of Readers in Hereford Diocese in October 2008. Having all too readily accepted the invitation I then discovered to my horror that on that particular weekend it would take five hours train travel in each direction to get there. And at quite short notice I was invited to go to a significant event in Thailand, related to my Anglican Communion work, which meant that I would only arrive home after a long flight on the Friday evening, and have to leave for Hereford early the next morning. All through the train journey to Hereford I was metaphorically cursing my own stupidity for getting myself into such a situation. When I eventually arrived I reflected with the group in Hereford on John 4 and made my comment about the difference in John's Gospel between the 'I am' sayings with a predicate such as 'I am the bread of life' – and these other – what I call the hidden 'I am' sayings. Then somebody pointed out that one way of translating John 4.26.could suggest that it too includes a predicate 'I am the one talking with you'. And that person was quite right. So just as Jesus is elsewhere describing God as the bread of life or the light of the world and identifying himself with those realities, so here he is describing God as 'the one talking with you' – and identifying himself with that expression of divinity. It is a powerful insight, which seems to suggest to me that the Gospel is saying that at the very heart of what it means to be God, as Jesus reveals it to us, is God's communication with humanity. It is of the very nature of God to be a God who communicates with his human creation. And this, I remind you, is the very first 'I am' of John's Gospel, so John is saying that this is the fundamental nature of God – upon which all the other things John wants to tell us about God in his Gospel will be based. It does of course link with the way that this Gospel opens with that profound meditation on the Word, the Logos. It is an insight that is surely difficult to grasp in its totality – but perhaps that is typical of the unpinnable-downness of the 'I am who I am'. So – to return to the personal reminiscence – I spent the train journey returning from Hereford saying to myself, 'It was worth making this journey just to gain that insight!'

What conclusions linked to our overall theme of reconciliation, do I draw from my exploration of these two passages in John's Gospel? How might these reflections impact on dialogue between Jews and Palestinians? I want to share three thoughts.

First, both Jews and Christians need to recover the biblical significance of what it means to call God 'I am who I am' and allow it to permeate and inform their religious consciousness. It may – and should – make a substantial difference to our engagement across religious or political boundaries. For the Western Christian it offers an alternative vision to the one that has dominated so many centuries of Jewish-Christian history, a history which ultimately bears a considerable share of responsibility for the current political situation in the Middle East. For the Jew, I would suggest that an exploration of God as 'I am' is a challenge to travel lightly with the baggage which may obstruct recognising God in the face of our neighbour, to recognise the God-becoming-present in the midst of uncomfortable conversation with one often thought of as 'the enemy', or perhaps even more subtly, 'the threat to my existence'. It also offers an implicit rebuke to certain Zionist theologies, whether Jewish or Christian, which seek to treat the Bible along the lines of a mathematical equation.

In the case of Palestinians, we need to recognise the variety of perspectives contained within the words 'Christian' and 'Muslim', for both religious traditions are very much present within the community, as well as that rather down-trodden and marginalised presence (at the moment) which might be defined as 'secular.' For the Christian Palestinian, in the 'I am' of Jesus, there may be the challenge to avoid the tempting literalism of running to embrace whole-heartedly a condemnation of Judaism and its heritage. For the 'I am' suggests the freedom to speak and to relate at a universal level. For the Muslim Palestinian, in the 'I am' of Jesus there may be a life-giving echo of something of the spiritual substance of the Qur'an, where God is known by one hundred names with one missing! Allah (God) is always beyond the terms of human entrapments. There is always more to the story, even when the story has been told to the best of human endeavours. And for the secular Palestinian, maybe agnostic or atheist, perhaps the Jesus of the 'I am' brings the hope that through compassionate human conversation a new future may be born.

Secondly, and linked closely to this, there is a profound

interplay (particularly in John 4) between the importance of particularity and universality. On the one hand there is Jesus' comment, 'Salvation is from the Jews' which stresses the importance of the specific, concrete and particular. On the other hand there is the challenge that this passage offers to the ideology of 'holy places', and the assertion 'God is Spirit, and those who worship him must worship in Spirit and in truth', which seem to suggest that to be confined by particularity is not enough, and can even be dangerous. In the context of today's Middle East in which the theological scandal of particularity can become truly scandalous we need to learn to discover ways of holding particularity and universality in a creative tension. It is no accident that the flashpoints for the underlying hostility in Israel/Palestine are so often linked to the control of and access to 'holy places'. In a number of ways the history between the Jews and Samaritans of New Testament times mirrors and reflects the hostility between the different religious groups involved in today's Israel/Palestine.

And finally, as I have already mentioned above the first time that Jesus speaks of his real nature it is to this woman, a member of a different religious community to his own, and a person of apparent ill repute. Might that just possibly be hinting to us that it is through our engagement with 'the other' that we can come to a truer revelation and understanding of who God that 'I am who I am' is, that God discloses himself to us in and through our relationship with people of other religious traditions? Is this part of what it might mean that Jesus' initial disclosure of himself is in the form 'I am the one talking to you'? And what would *this* mean for the peoples of the Middle East Jews, Christians and Muslims?

---

[1] See for example the following passage from the Samaritan Memar Marqah, which intriguingly picks up the symbol of 'water of life'

found also as a central theme in John 4. It is difficult however to make definite assertions as to what exactly the Samaritans believed during the New Testament times, as all the extant sources (including the Memar Marqah) come from several centuries later.

> Lifted up is Moses, the great Prophet,
> whom his Lord clothed with his name [cf. Exod 7:1]!
> He dwelt in hidden things and was surrounded with Light.
> The Truth was revealed to him and he gave him the writing of his own hand.
> He gave him to drink from ten precious springs, seven above and three below.
> Deity drew for him the waters of Life [mayah chayyah]
> which watered his heart, until it produced that which gives life.
> Prophecy drew for him the waters of Life which purified his soul, until it made every soul great.
> Truth drew for him the waters of Life which made his spirit great, until it was able to illumine.
> And the four Names [of God]* drew for him the waters of life, so that he might be lifted up and glorified in every place. ---
> Marqah, *Memar* 2.9, 12
> Quoted from
> http://www.bible-history.com/Samaritans/SAMARITANSTheir_Religion.htm

Bibliography

Ackroyd, Peter (1995) *Blake*. London: Sinclair-Stevenson.
Abbott, W., Gallagher, J. (eds) (1966), *The Documents of Vatican II*. London: Chapman.
Aristotle (1972) *The Politics*. Trans. T.A. Sinclair. Harmondsworth: Penguin.
Ateek, Naim Stefan (2008) *A Palestinian Christian Cry for Reconciliation*. Maryknoll, NY: Orbis.
Banfield, Stephen (1989) *Sensibility and English Song: Critical Studies of the Early Twentieth Century.* 2 vols. Cambridge: Cambridge University Press.
Barthes, Roland (1957) *Mythologies.* Seuil: Paris.
Bar-Josef, Eitan (2005) *The Holy Land in English Culture 1799-1917: Palestine and the Question of Orientalism*. Oxford: Oxford University Press.
Benjamin, W. (first published 1950) "Theses on the Philosophy of History", in Arendt, H. ed. (1970) trans. Zohn, H. *Illuminations*, New York: Schocken.
Berkovitz, E. (1978) "Facing the Truth, *Judaism* 27.
Brown, Raymond (1975) 'The Passion According to John: Chapters 18 and 19', Brudholm, T. (2008) *Resentment's Virtue, Jean Amery and the refusal to forgive.* Philadelphia: Temple Press.
Burke (1790) Reflections on the Revolution in France. Pall Mall: J. Dodsley.
Burkert, Walter (1972) *Homo Necans.* Berlin: Walter de Gruyter & Co.
Butler (1726) *Sermons Preached at the Rolls Chapel*. London: J&J Knapton.
Cavanaugh, William T. (2005) 'Killing for the telephone company.

Why the nation-state is not the keeper of the common good', in McCann, D.P. and Miller, P.D. ed. (2005) *In Search of the Common Good*. New York, London: T&T Clark.

Clausewitz (1937) *Vom Kriege*. Hamburg.

Colles, H.C. (1942) *Walford Davies: a Biography*. London: Oxford University Press.

Crick, Bernard (1982) *In Defence of Politics*. 2nd edition 1982. Harmondsworth: Pelican.

Crossley. James G. (2008) *Jesus in an Age of Terror*. London: Equinox.

Dearmer, Percy (1925) *Songs of Praise*. London: Oxford University Press, no. 204; enlarged edition, 1931, no. 446.

Dearmer, Percy (1933) *Songs of Praise Discussed*. London: Oxford University Press.

Dibble, Jeremy (1992) *C. Hubert Parry: His Life and Music*. Oxford: Clarendon Press.

Erdman, David V. (ed) (1981) *The Complete Poetry and Prose of William Blake*. Berkeley, CA: University of California Press.

Duff, Nancy J. 'The Commandments and the Common Life – Reflections on Paul

Fawcett, M.G. (1924) *What I Remember*. London: Unwin.

For the Right: Essays and Addresses by Members of the "Fight for Right" Movement (with a preface by Sir Francis Younghusband) (1918) New York and London: Freudman, Lillian C. (1994) *Anti-Semitism in the New Testament*. MD: UPA.

G. P. Putnam's Sons.

Fukuyama, Francis (1992) *The End of History and the Last Man*. Washington D.C.: The National Interest

Gergen, K (1999) *An Invitation to Social Constructionism*. London: Sage.

Gibran, K. (1992) The *Prophet*. London: Pan Books.

Gibson, Lorna (2006), 'The Women's Institute and *Jerusalem's* Suffrage Past' in *Women's History Review* 15, 323-335

Girard, R. (1972) *Violence et le Sacré* trans. Patrick Gregory (2005)

Violence and the Sacred. London / New York: Continuum.

Graves, C.L. (1926) *Hubert Parry: His Life and Works*, 2 vols. London: Macmillan.

Griswold, Charles (2007) *Forgiveness, A Philosophical Exploration*. Cambridge: Cambridge University Press.

Guthrie, C. and Quinlan, M. (2007) *The Just War Tradition: Ethics in Modern Warfare*. London: Bloomsbury.

Hauerwas, S., Willimon, W. (1989) *Resident Aliens: Life in the Christian Colony*. Nashville: Abingdon.

Hauerwas. S. (2010) *Hannah's Child: A Theologian's Memoir*. London: SCM Press.

Hicks, J. (1994) *Reason and Christian Religion*. Oxford: Clarendon.

Hobsbawm, E.J. (1962) *The Age of Revolution: 1789-1848*. London: Weidenfeld & Nicolson.

Hobsbawm, E.J. (1975) *The Age of Capital: 1848-1875*. London: Weidenfeld & Nicolson.

Hobsbawm, E.J. (1987) *The Age of Empire: 1875-1914*. London: Weidenfeld & Nicolson.

Hobsbawm, E.J. (1995) The Age of Extremes: the short twentieth century, 1914-1991. London: Abacus Book.

Homer (1924) *The Iliad* trans. A.T. Murray. London: Loeb Classical Library.

Howard, Michael (2002) *Peace and War*. London: Athenaeum.

Kant, I. (1996) *The Metaphysics of Morals.* Cambridge: Cambridge University Press.

Kant, I. (1790) *The Science of Right,* available online at http://ebooks.adelaide.edu.au/k/kant/immanuel/k16sr/

Kennedy, Michael (1968) *Portrait of Elgar.* Oxford: Oxford University Press.

Lehmann's *The Decalogue and a Human Future'* in Ziegler, P.G. and Bartel, M.J. eds. (2009) *Explorations in Christian Theology and Ethics: Essays in Conversation with Paul L. Lehmann*. Farnham, Surrey: Ashgate, pp. 29-44.

Lehmann, Paul L. (1940) *Forgiveness: Decisive Issue in Protestant Thought.* New York: Harper & Brothers.

Lehmann, Paul L. (1963) *Ethics in a Christian Context.* New York: Harper & Row.

Lehmann, Paul L. (1975) *The Transfiguration of Politics: The Presence and Power of Jesus of Nazareth in and over Human Affairs.* New York: Harper & Row.

Lehmann, Paul L. (1995) *The Decalogue and A Human Future: The Meaning of the Commandments for Making and Keeping Life Human.* Grand Rapids: Eerdmans.

Looker, Ben (2002) *Exhibiting Imperial London: empire and the city in late Victorian and Edwardian guidebooks.* London: Goldsmiths College.

MacIntyre, Alisdair (1984) *After Virtue. A Study in Moral Theory.* 2nd edition. Notre Dame, Indiana: University of Notre Dame Press.

MacIntyre, Alisdair (1990) *Three Rival Versions of Moral Enquiry. Encyclopaedia, Genealogy, and Tradition.* London: Duckworth.

MacIntyre, Alisdair (2009) 'Intractable Moral Disagreements' in Cunningham, L.S. ed. (2009) *Intractable Disputes about the Natural Law. Alasdair MacIntyre and Critics.* Notre Dame, Ind.: University of Notre Dame Press. pp. 1-52.

Maistre, Joseph de (1797) ed. Lebrun, Richard A. (1994) *Considerations on France.*
Cambridge: CUP.

Mali, J. (1992) The Rehabilitation of Myth: Vico's New Science. Cambridge: CUP.

Markay, David (2009) "A Parable" under section Reflection, Corrymeela, Vol 9, No 3 December 2009.

Milman, Henry Hart (1863) *History of the Jews* 2 vols, London: John Murray, third edition.

Murphy, J.G. (2009) *Mercy and legal Justice.* Cambridge: CUP.

Orens, John Richard (2003) *Stewart Headlam's Radical Anglicanism:*

The Mass, the Masses, and the Music Hall. Urbana and Chicago: University of Chicago Press.

Peterson, Eugene H. (2005) *Christ Plays in Ten Thousand Places*. London: Hodder & Stoughton.

Philo and Berry (2004) *Bad News From Israel*. London: Pluto Press

Porter, J. 'Does the Natural Law Provide a Universally Valid Morality?' in Cunningham, L.S. ed. (2009) *Intractable Disputes about the Natural Law. Alisdair MacIntyre and Critics.* Notre Dame, Ind.: University of Notre Dame Press. pp. 53–95.

Potter, J (1996) *Representing Reality: Discourse, Rhetoric and Social Construction*. London: Sage.

Price, Reynolds (1996) *Three Gospels*. New York: Screibner.

Quarterly Meeting of the Palestine Exploration Fund. (1875) London: Bentley.

Reeves, M, Worsley, J (2001) Favourite Hymns: Two Hundred Years of Magnificat. London: Continuum

Rollins, Peter (2006) *How (Not) to Speak of God*. London: SCM Press

Rubinstein, David (1991) *A different world for women: the life of Millicent Garrett Fawcett.* Columbus: Ohio State University Press.

Ruether, Rosemary Radford (1974) *Faith and Fratricide: the theological roots of anti-Semitism*. New York: Seabury.

Ruston, R. (2004) *Human Rights and the image of God*. London: SCM Press.

Sacks, J. (2002) *The Dignity of Difference*. London: Continuum.

Schellenberg, James A. (1982) *The Science of Conflict*. Oxford: Oxford University Press.

Schorr, Samuel (1907) *Palestine in London: Official Guide.* London: London Society for Promoting Christianity Amongst the Jews.

Stanley, Arthur Penhryn (1856) *Sinai and Palestine in Connection with their History*. London: Murray, third edition.

Swinburne, R. (1989) *Responsibility and Atonement*. Oxford: Clarendon.

Taylor, Charles (1997) 'The Politics of Recognition', *Philosophical Arguments*. Cambridge, Mass.: Harvard University Press.

Vanier, Jean (2004) *Drawn into the mystery of Jesus through the Gospel of John*. London: DLT.

Verene, D.P. (1981) *Vico's Science of Imagination*. Ithaca: Cornell.

Vico, G. (1999) *New Science*, trans. D. Marsh. Harmondsworth: Penguin.

Weber, Max (1919) 'Politics as a Vocation' in Gerth, H.H. and Mills, C.W. trans. and eds. (1948) *Max Weber*. London: Routledge & Kegan Paul.

Wren, Brian A. (1973) "Deep in the Shadows of the Past" in
Methodist Publishing House (1983) *Hymns and Psalms*. Avon: Bath Press.

Wright, N.T. (1996) *Jesus and the Victory of God*. London: SPCK.

Wright, N.T. (2000) *The Challenge of Jesus*. London: SPCK, 2000.

Zimmerli, Walther (1978) *Old Testament Theology in Outline*. London: T&T Clark.